A Catholic Marries a Hindu

Also by Paul Bouchard

A Package at Gitmo
The Boy Who Wanted to Be a Man
Enlistment

A Catholic Marries a Hindu

Paul Bouchard

iUniverse, Inc.
Bloomington

A Catholic Marries a Hindu

iUniverse books may be ordered through booksellers or by contacting:

iUniverse
1663 Liberty Drive
Bloomington, IN 47403
www.iuniverse.com
1-800-Authors (1-800-288-4677)

ISBN: 978-1-4759-3734-3 (sc)
ISBN: 978-1-4759-3737-4 (ebk)

Printed in the United States of America

iUniverse rev. date: 09/27/2012

To my goddess of wealth

I think it would be a good idea.

Mahatma Gandhi, when a reporter asked for his thoughts on Western civilization

CONTENTS

PREFACE

Writers are constantly looking for stories to write, and I'm no different—I'm always thinking of subjects to write about. Truth be told, I've always been one to adhere to the popular advice often given to writers about their craft—write what you know and know what you write.

It was from the intersection of these two forces—my constant search for stories and my desire to write something I knew something about—that I decided to write about how I came to know, love, and marry my wife, Latika.

It was actually shortly after our marriage in August 2004 when I really began to think seriously about writing this book. Over the years, I jotted down notes about our relationship, notes about things I wanted to write about, and things that could be broadly described as "cultural differences." That, if anything, is what this book is really about—how two people from different backgrounds, very different parts of the world, very different cultures, and very different religious traditions, came to know each other, fall in love, and get married.

Latika Sreenivasulu, my wife, was born in 1971 in Bombay (Mumbai), India, but grew up in Madras (Chennai). Madras is India's fourth-largest city. It has a population of four million, double that if one considers the greater metropolitan area. Located on the coast of the Bay of Bengal, Madras has a hot and humid climate, and it is sometimes referred to as the "Detroit of India" because a lot of India's car manufacturing takes place there. Crowded with people, Madras' streets are also lined with open-air shops, and merchants pushing their products and produce in small wheeled carts are a familiar sight. Lastly, Madras is cosmopolitan, but its people are mainly Hindus, and the languages spoken are numerous indeed.

Then there's me. I was born in 1967 and raised in Frenchville, Maine, population two thousand. Frenchville has cold and long winters, tons of snow, numerous potato fields, no traffic to speak of, no crowds, and no open-air markets. It is some two hundred miles from Maine's famous rocky coast. Indeed, Frenchville is located on the upper banks of the St. John River, the river that, in part, serves as the United States-Canada international border. The people of Frenchville are Catholics. The languages spoken are English and French, with the latter dying a slow death.

Madras and Frenchville are truly worlds and oceans apart. It is truly East meets West. How did Latika from Madras and I from Frenchville come to know each other, fall in love, and eventually marry? That, too, is what this book is about.

For privacy reasons, I've changed the names of certain individuals. Also, there's a bit about religion in this book, but not much. Simply put, I thought the title, *A Catholic Marries a Hindu*, fit well and hit upon the main theme of cultural differences.

Lastly and, most importantly, in no way do I profess to be some type of expert on India, Indians, and Hinduism. Undoubtedly, there are experts in these cultural differences fields, and their academic training is usually in disciplines like sociology, history, or cultural anthropology. I don't have those academic credentials, but what I do have is a background in international relations and law, and I have experiences and general observations. It is these experiences and general observations that I share with the reader. I hope readers will enjoy these experiences and observations of mine. I know I had fun writing about them.

Paul Bouchard
El Paso, Texas
June 2009

ACKNOWLEDGMENTS

To Terri Sirois, Ryan Little, Cory Kneeland, Racy Haddad, Jennifer Doak, Carla Arpa, Gerry Morin, John and Meena Allen, Brian Collin, Dave Howey, Brian Mathison, Nevena and Brad Bentz, Robert Barnsby, and Charlie McElroy. These friends encouraged me to keep writing. Thanks, guys.

CHAPTER ONE

Hooking Up

It was December 2001, a couple days before Christmas. That was the first time I met my future wife, Latika. I was a second-year law student at Texas Tech University School of Law in Lubbock. I was also a member of a local National Guard unit, the 2-142 (2nd Battalion, 142nd Infantry, Mechanized), also based out of Lubbock.

Some four months prior was that awful day in American history, September 11, the day Al-Qaeda-backed terrorists attacked our country and the loss of life numbered around three thousand. Then shortly after, sometime in mid-October, my National Guard unit's first sergeant called me.

The first sergeant said, "Sergeant Bouchard, we need twenty-four soldiers to pull airport security in Lubbock and Amarillo. You're one of the twenty-four I'm picking."

"Roger that, Top."[1]

Truth be told, I was glad to be selected for this mission.

Our nation was recently attacked. I'm in the National Guard. Let me do my thing, was my thinking.

At first, I thought I'd be on the Lubbock security team, pulling security around Lubbock Airport, but I was placed on the Amarillo security team. Simply put, the hours of our work shifts, coupled with the geographic distance between Amarillo and Lubbock (the drive takes some two hours), forced me to drop out of law school for that semester. That was no big deal, especially because I knew my short mission stint would end in late December, which it did.

* * *

---

[1]   First sergeants are often referred to as "Top."

Prema and Bill Johnson were some of the first students I met at Texas Tech when I began law school there in the fall of 2000. They were friendly and pleasant folks, a nice couple, and good parents to their two children. The three of us soon became friends, and part of our unwritten routine was for them to invite me over to their apartment about once a month. This routine usually took place on a Friday or Saturday night. Prema, who is originally from India, would often cook Indian food. After dinner, we'd all watch a movie.

Now it was late December 2001. I had just finished my stint on that security mission, and I was back in Lubbock. The phone rang. It was Prema, inviting me over for dinner.

"Oh, and my sisters will be visiting, Paul. They'll be visiting us for Christmas," she said. "Come have dinner with us. You'll meet my sisters."

I did.

The dinner was like a regular dinner at Prema's and Bill's apartment. We ate Indian food and we watched a movie. Bill and I talked about upcoming law classes, the professors teaching those courses, America's response to September 11, and other political and economic issues of the time.

That's what I remember most about that evening-eating, watching a movie, and talking to Bill, the conversation mostly being about politics. Later in the evening, I was indeed introduced to Prema's three sisters. I did the correct social graces thing. I said "hello" and shook their hands.

"I'm Paul. Nice to meet you."

And that was it. I'm so bad with names—I forgot the names of her three sisters probably in ten minutes or less. What I do remember was that the sisters were nice and cordial, and they were all PhD students at New Mexico State University in Las Cruces where they all shared an apartment.

*   *   *

The spring semester began in January 2002, and during the first week of classes, Prema came up to me while I was in the law school break room. I was drinking coffee.

"Paul, did you have a good time at our last dinner about two weeks ago?"

"Sure, of course," I said.

There was a brief pause.

"Would it be okay for one of my sisters, Latika, to give you her phone number and e-mail address?"

"Sure, of course."

"Great."

She proceeded to give me Latika's telephone number and e-mail address.

Now which one of the three sisters was Latika?

I began to correspond with Latika almost immediately after receiving her contact information. Looking back, I'd say I'd call or e-mail her once a week. Our weekly calls and e-mails weren't elaborate. They were short and friendly.

What are you up to? How's it going? How are your classes going? When will you be done with your PhD program? How are your sisters doing?

*   *   *

Fast forward to May of 2002. My National Guard unit was again activated, and we were training at Fort Hood, Texas, getting ready for an upcoming deployment to Guantanamo Bay, Cuba, or Gitmo for short.

Our unit's training at Fort Hood was going well. Wake up was around 5:00 AM, AND from that time until 4:30 PM, it was train, train, train. Then came dinner and downtime, time to prepare uniforms, shine boots, relax, make phone calls, and so forth. My practice was to go for a light jog during downtime, and then I'd shower, prepare my uniform for the next day's training, and make any phone calls to friends.

It was during one of these phone calls that my friendship to Latika went up a notch or two. Actually, our friendship went up many notches during that fateful call because it crossed that important threshold line, that line where a friendship turns into a bona fide relationship.

"Well, Paul, am I just one of your girls? A girl you just keep in touch with?" Latika asked during that all-important conversation in May 2002.

"Well . . . uh . . . what do you mean?"

"Well, I want something more serious." Her tone was serious, too.

These typical calls to friends lasted, at most, five minutes, but this particular conversation with Latika lasted much longer. And from that point on, my phone calls and e-mails to Latika became more serious—they lasted longer, and the topics of conversation often involved what *we* had in mind for the future and what *our* plans were. We really got to know each other.

One can actually fall in love with someone else when the means of communication is a phone line, be it a regular phone or the Internet. That's how it started with Latika and me—our courtship started via a phone line. The more I contacted her, the more I realized I was in a relationship with someone who was beautiful, interesting, and serious. And once I got to Gitmo, my e-mails and phone calls to her didn't subside. If anything, they picked up even if my cell phone couldn't find a signal in Cuba.[2] Latika and I were falling in love.

*   *   *

My courtship of Latika was brief partly because I fell in love with her quickly, but another factor was, in my opinion, a cultural thing. Indians are generally serious people who get right to the issue at hand.

The next chapter discusses this phenomenon. I argue this seriousness largely applies to career and work issues, but it also applies to dating and marriage. The fact is, Indians often don't date much—they go right to tying the knot. I discuss this later in chapter three.

Truth be told, if Latika had her way, our courtship would have been even shorter, and we would have married sooner.

---

[2]   We did have pay phones at Gitmo.

CHAPTER TWO

Cultural Differences

Prior to meeting Prema and Latika, I knew very few Indians. My sister had actually dated an Indian man once, and I had met him a couple times. Also, I remember one graduate school classmate of mine was from India. He was very smart and thin as a rail. He smoked like a chimney, too. Then at Gitmo, I had seen Indians, too, but I really didn't know them. The Indians I saw at Gitmo were migrant workers working for a Halliburton subsidiary. I wrote about these migrant workers briefly in one of my novellas, *A Package at Gitmo*. In it, I wrote that:

- The Jamaican migrant workers were big, tall, jovial types who were often smiling and laughing aloud.
- The Filipino migrant workers were all short and pudgy, and they also smiled and laughed often.
- The Indian and Pakistani migrant workers were overwhelmingly short and thin, and I never saw any of them smile or laugh.

What follows are my general observations of Indians. No doubt, I'm not an expert on the subject, and I approach the matter from my background, a Western perspective, an American perspective. Thus, in the end, it's a comparative analysis—an American observing Indians from an American perspective.

What prompted this comparative analysis was that I noticed many things mycourtship and eventual marriage to Latika, and I often couldn't help but wonder at times:

Does she do this, say that, or have this particular attitude because of her cultural background? Because she's from India? Because she's Indian?

I still wonder about this sometimes, and the next section may shed some light on the subject.

A Typical Conversation in the Workplace in America

Let's say there's a conversation between Bob and Mark. Bob and Mark, both in their mid-thirties, are Americans and lawyers in a midsized law firm. Bob is married, and he has two children while Mark recently broke up with his girlfriend, Laura. It's Monday morning, and Bob and Mark meet up in the break room of the law firm. It's eight o'clock. The two are having their morning coffee.

"Mark buddy, how's it hanging? How was your weekend?"

"Hi, Bob. Mornin' to ya. I had a nice weekend. I hit a few golf balls yesterday. That was fun. I had a nice date on Saturday night, too. Name's Julie. She's hot, man, lemme tell ya. Met her online. I'm taking it slow, of course. You know I recently broke up with Laura. How was your weekend, slugger?"

"Not bad. Carol went to visit her folks in Pittsburgh. Her dad's fighting cancer, you know. I had the kids for the weekend."

"Oh, I see."

"Yeah. John had a Little League game on Saturday. Kid went two for four, too. That was at eleven o'clock. Then my youngest, Anne, had a soccer game. That was at two o'clock. I tell you, buddy, kids are a lot of work."

"I can see that."

"And I worked on my old BMW yesterday. Thing's ancient, but it still runs well. Got more than three hundred thousand miles on the old bugger."

"You don't say."

"Yep. It's making some funny noise though. I'm thinking I'll have to bring it to the shop. I'm mechanical, but I'm not that mechanical. I'm also thinking of giving it a new paint job. I'm tired of red. I want my old BMW to be black. What ya think?"

"Cool. Black's cool. I'd go black."

"Yeah, see, it was Carol's car for a long time. She liked it red, but I'm thinking black, especially now that I'm driving it more."

There's a brief pause as the two sip from their coffees.

Bob asks, "How 'bout them Red Sox, huh? Check the game last night? Beckett threw a shutout. You know, since I grew up in New England, I'm definitely part of that Red Sox nation."

"Yeah yeah, don't remind me." Mark says, rolling his eyes. "I know you're with the Red Sox. My poor Royals are borderline in the cellar."

"Sorry, man. Heck, I remember when you guys were a powerhouse. Back in them George Brett/Darrel Porter days. Kansas City used to kick some major ass."

"Yeah, but those days are long gone. We haven't done shit in a long time."

A few quiet seconds pass as the two continue to sip their coffees.

"Fuckin' contractors, man," Bob suddenly says. "That's one thing that also happened this weekend."

"What's that?"

"Oh, we've got a leak coming from our kitchen ceiling. Took me almost two months to find a contractor who'd finally give me a bid. Dude wants $1,200. It's a rip-off, Mark, lemme tell ya."

"Yeah, sounds high dollar if you ask me."

"Got that right, buddy. Anyway, my brother-in-law is in the business. Maybe I can talk him into doing it for fewer bucks."

There's more quiet time and more coffee-sipping.

"Hey, how's that Johnson case shaking?" Bob asks. "Any amount on the table?"

"Nah. Insurance company is willing to settle for $13,000. Fuckin' neighbor's dog bit her. Minor injuries if you ask me, but Ms. Johnson thinks she can get more than that. I'm telling ya, Bob, I sometimes have a harder time with my clients than the insurance companies I'm fighting against."

"I hear you, bud. Sounds like my Rodriguez case. Tough client. No budging. Looks like we're going to court."

There' s silence for a few seconds.

Bob says, "Got some sad news, pal. Don't think Fluffy's gonna make it."

"Oh no," says Mark, genuinely concerned.

"Yeah, poor dog's twelve years old and in poor health."

"Sorry to hear that."

"Carol knows, but she doesn't know how serious it is. I brought Fluffy to the vet on Saturday. The dog is costing me a fortune in vet bills, but we've had her since she was a puppy. I think we'll have to put her to sleep."

"Sorry to hear that."

There's a long pause. Mark shifts gears.

"You know, man, if I don't make partner in two years, then I'm hanging my own shingle. Fuck it. I'll strike it out on my own. The law office of Mark Brenner. What ya think?"

"Sounds like a winner. Shit, maybe I'll work for you. The way my work evaluations are going, it looks like I'll need a miracle to make partner."

Suddenly, Wendy, one of the law firm's partners, walks into the break room. "Mornin', fellas. How's everyone doing this fine Monday morning?"

"Splendid." Bob says. smiling.

"Couldn't be better."

"I got donuts for everyone." Wendy places a tray of donuts on the table. "Help yourselves."

"Well, there goes my diet," says Mark. "Carb attack, here I come."

"What's the special occasion, Wendy? I've never seen you bring donuts."

"Well, my youngest, Jessica, won a spelling bee contest on Friday. She'll compete in the regionals next week, so I thought we could all celebrate."

"Cool," says Bob.

Bob and Mark each grab a donut. A few quiet seconds pass.

Bob says, "Hey, listen, Mark. Carol's coming back tomorrow. What you say you and . . . What's your new girlfriend's name?"

"Julie. She's not my girlfriend, at least not yet. We've only had one date."

"Right. What you say you and Julie come over to our place on Wednesday night? We'll do steaks on the grill. Steak and beer. BoSox are on ESPN, too. Beer and steaks, bud. And Carol and I would like to meet Julie. What do you say? Oh, you can come, too, Wendy. Carol's great at spelling. She'll practice with Jessica."

Analysis of the Conversation Highlighting the Differences between Americans and Indians

Language

Notice the tone and manner of American English:

+ Hey, buddy.
+ Hey, man.
+ What's up, dude?
+ Hi, slugger.

- ◆ Cool.
- ◆ Sounds like a winner.
- ◆ Ah, shit.

There's a lot of slang in American English, and it's increasingly not just teenage kids or college students who speak it. And "fuck" is also quite popular in the American vernacular, even when talking in front of one's supervisor.

Slang, in my opinion, also highlights another common American characteristic, that of individuality and informality because, at the heart of American thinking and character, is the individual, not the state, nation, and family. The individual is the center of everything. I . . . Me. I'll discuss these themes later, but I'll argue our language and how we speak it goes to this individual-as-the-center theme.

Indians, in comparison, are much more serious, so they speak in a more formal tone with no slang. They also, in my opinion, sometimes speak very fast. My first telephone conversations with Latika were awkward because she spoke fast and I wasn't catching everything in the conversation. She also spoke in a more formal tone which took a little getting used to. I also found myself cutting back on the slang.

In no way am I suggesting a language barrier here because Indians in America, overall, do very well and they are understood when they speak. They just sometimes need to slow it down, and I think that, the longer they're here in America, the more apt they are to speak English slower. And as to the informality of American slang, that is also easy to pick up and adapt into one's manner of speaking. If you bring an Indian to America, in two or three months, he will be incorporating American slang into his vocabulary.

I'll highlight a few examples of differences between American English and Indian English:

American	Indian
♦ "Let me say this."	♦ "I tell you this." ♦ "This I tell you."
♦ "Turn off the light." ♦ "Shut the light."	♦ "Off the light."
♦ "Give me a roll of film."	♦ "Give me a film roll."

I did a double take the first time I heard Latika say, "Pass me a film roll, Paul." It took me a few seconds to figure it out. "We say film roll, Paul, not a roll of film." How can I argue? India has more English speakers than we do here in the United States. Film roll it is.

"Here's your film roll, honey."

Coffee versus tea

Bob, Mark, and Wendy were having a coffee break. Americans are mostly coffee drinkers while Indians tend to prefer hot tea over coffee. And Latika has often reminded me that Indians aren't too used to decaffeinated drinks, mochas, and all the other extras that come with American coffee such as whipcream.

Small talk

Notice the topics of conversation among Bob, Mark, and Wendy: sports, pets, a paint job for a car, a house repair, and a child's spelling bee competition. It's all small talk.

Indians, in my opinion, are serious people and serious people have difficulty with small talk. Big political subjects, world topics, and work-related stuff, there are no issues there, but small talk like what fertilizer to use on one's lawn or how one's child is doing in basketball is hard for serious people to engage in. Let's take the small talk topics one-by-one.

♦ **Sports.** In the United States, sports often become a topic of conversation in the workplace. Besides cricket, Indians don't talk much about sports. And forget the whole issue of college sports or sports for kids. Indian college students go to college to study, not to play sports. The same is true of Indian schoolchildren because they also focus on academics rather than athletics. The idea of organized sports leagues for kids in India is nowhere to the level it is here in the United States, and it's certainly not a topic Indian parents engage in and discuss in the workplace.

♦ **Paint job for a car.** Bob wanted his BMW to be black and not red. I believe this wouldn't be a topic of discussion among Indians because America is a car nation and Indian is not . . . not yet anyway. Cars are the means of transportation in the United States. Several large cities have good public transit systems, but cars are unquestionably the primary means of transport. In India, trains, buses, bikes, and taxis are how people are transported. Indeed, Indians moving to America have to make this transportation adjustment, and they do. Latika, for instance, didn't know how to drive a car until she came to the United States. Also, talking about a new paint job for one's car because one doesn't like its color isn't something an Indian would talk about. An Indian would likely think, "The car is red. That's fine. Big deal." And even if the Indian got a paint job for his car, he probably wouldn't talk about it. Indians can be secretive—they use a lot of discretion about what they talk about and who they are talking with.

♦ **Pets.** Americans love pets, especially cats and dogs. Pets are a big deal in the United States, and pet owners spend a considerable amount of money on their pets—pet food, grooming, shots and vaccines, and so forth. We even have pet cemeteries, and some pet owners have provisions in their wills that cover their pets. India is not a pet nation. Latika is actually afraid of cats, dogs, and animals in general. Based on my observations, Indians generally don't have pets, so it's not something they talk about.

♦ **House repairs.** Homes are a big topic of discussion in America. General repairs, remodeling the kitchen, and a new fertilizer for that all-important lawn, Americans talk about this stuff a lot. Indians? Not so much. Again, Indians don't engage in too much small talk.

♦ **Children.** Bob and Wendy talked considerably about their kids, and this again goes to the theme of the "individual as center." Individualism is the American way; American kids are encouraged to think on their own and develop into the person they want to become. Common and popular sayings in America include:

+ Be all you can be.
+ The sky's the limit.
+ You can be anything you want.
+ Reach for the stars.
+ I'm number one.

America, compared to many other countries, is a young, forward-looking nation. We do have a history of accepting peoples from all over the world, but, once they're here, they're American. To be an American means you're in charge. You're in charge of your own destiny. What one studies in college, what career one pursues, and who one chooses to marry, I, as the individual, decide this. Sure, there are family pressures and expectations at times, but the idea that one decides for himself rings true in America, and it starts at an early age.

+ "Do you want to go to baseball or soccer camp this summer?"
+ "Mommy and Daddy will buy you a bike. What color do you want?"
+ "Do you want to take piano or ballerina lessons?"
+ "What do you want for dinner? French fries? Okay, Mommy will cook you French fries."

Children in America often have these decisions to make, and parents will quite often oblige. True, not every American child is raised this way, but many are. And American kids—again with individualism and the authority that comes with it—can talk back to their parents.

"No, Mommy, I disagree."

"Why not? Why can't I have one?"

"Dad, you're wrong. I think . . ."

It's not that children in America are all undisciplined and constantly arguing with their parents, but individualism, which is at the heart of American culture, is often at play, and it starts early.

My two favorite Indian movies are *The Namesake* and *Slumdog Millionaire*. For now, let me just use a scene from *The Namesake*, the one where the little boy decides to change his name. In the movie, the little boy, whose parents are from India, is given an Indian first name. For whatever reason, he decides to change his first name. Interestingly, in that scene, his mother remarks something to the effect, "In America, it is the children who decide their names."

On occasion, Latika has told me that this thing about children having choices, being given choices, developing an independent mind, talking and discussing with their parents as equals, and sometimes (if need be) even disagreeing and talking back to their parents is absolutely unheard of in India. It simply doesn't happen. For example, decisions such as what career one pursues, where one will live, and who one will marry—a combination of culture and family and parents will decide that.

♦ **Old age and death.** On the opposite end of children and youth is the issue of old age and, eventually, death. This topic forces me to think back about the time I watched the successful writer and speaker, D'Nesh D'Souza, on C-SPAN. D'Souza, who was born in India, came to the United States as a high school exchange student, went to college here, and eventually worked in the Reagan administration. He's a keen observer of political, social, and cultural issues. At times, he speaks about the differences between India and the United States to highlight whatever point or argument he's trying to make. On that particular episode, D'Souza spoke about how funerals in India are a big deal as compared to funerals in America. When one dies in India, not only do family members come to pay their last respects, but just about everyone who knew the deceased shows up for the funeral. Hundreds, sometimes even a thousand people, are present at a funeral. Also, in India, a family mourns the deceased for an entire year immediately following the death of the deceased, and in that mourning period, no one celebrates a holiday or even a birthday—everyone mourns. Here in America, family members and relatives usually attend funerals.

We mourn, and we're sad, but we move on. And we certainly don't officially mourn for a year.

♦ **Social invitations.** Bob invited both Mark and Wendy over for barbecue. Bob is actually a subordinate of Wendy, a partner in the law firm. In India, an employee would never invite a superior to his home for a social gathering because authority lines and rules governing social graces are strictly defined and adhered to in India. In India, people know their place in society, and an employee just doesn't invite the boss over. Also notice how Bob invites Julie over for the same barbecue. Bob has never met Julie, yet he invites her over for barbecue just the same. Latika is very uncomfortable going to other peoples' homes when she doesn't know the hosts. The fact that Bob invites Julie over—coupled with the fact that Julie will probably accept his invitation—simply wouldn't take place in India. Latika doesn't invite people in our home she doesn't know, and she so rarely accepts invitations from hosts she doesn't know either.

♦ **Open discussions.** For an Indian, the conversation between Bob, Mark, and Wendy has an air of openness and informality that is hard to comprehend. First, everyone is speaking to each other on a first-name basis. Even Bob and Mark refer to Wendy by her first name. Also consider the degree of openness and frankness in the conversation. That is also hard for Indians to comprehend. Notice Bob mentioning how his father-in-law is battling cancer; notice how Mark reveals he may quit the law firm if he sees he won't make partner in time. True, not every American would discuss and reveal such issues if they didn't know the person they were talking to, but, compared to Indians (and probably other peoples of other nationalities), Americans are fairly open and frank about what they discuss to others:

  ♦ "I spent $4,000 repairing my roof this past weekend."
  ♦ "My father-in-law died, and my wife Susan inherited $50,000."
  ♦ "I traded in my Chevy Malibu over the weekend for a newer model."

Americans reveal such things to one another, and the parties don't necessarily have to be close friends either because Americans will sometimes reveal such things to strangers, too. Indians would not reveal such things in their conversations.

♦ **Alcohol.** The planned barbecue will include beer. Indians, for the most part, do not drink alcoholic beverages. They also don't eat pork because they consider pigs dirty, and they don't eat beef because cows, for Hindus, are considered sacred. Surprisingly, many Indian restaurants I've been to serve beer and wine, but it's true that I hardly ever see Indians, especially Indian women, consuming alcohol. It's also surprising that a former British colony wouldn't have a drinking tradition, especially since India brews great beer—Kingfisher and Taj Mahal are two brands that come to mind. I guess I'll just leave it at that: Indians make great beer; they simply don't have a tradition of drinking it.

What I've Learned about India from My Wife

This section includes my general observations of and experiences with Indians. I've also consulted a few books on the particular area of inquiry I'm writing about.

Importantly, I've always tried to adhere to the general tenet of logic that states, "You can't go from the general to the particular, nor can you go from the particular to the general." That tenet is very true, of course, because, for example, one shouldn't say, "Bob is from the American Samoan Islands. Bob is tall, so all men from the American Samoan Islands are tall." Nor can one say, "Men from the American Samoan Islands are generally tall, and Bob is from the American Samoan Islands, so Bob must be tall."

It's just like the topic of alcohol previously mentioned. Indians in general don't drink alcohol, but that doesn't mean you can't find an Indian drinking a beer or some wine. The rule of logic is simple. Keep generalities as generalities, and keep what's particular to a person to that one person.

What follows are my opinions (my generalities) about India and its people. Inevitably, seeing such generalities through my American and Western perspective means I'm using my country, the United States, as a basis of comparison.

15

Seriousness

By serious, I mean that Indians work very hard, and I believe many Indians think that life is essentially about work. Two other generalities are associated with this generality of Indians being a serious people:

- Indians are not a fun-loving, humorous people.
- Indians tend to be very money-oriented. (Work hard. Don't have too much fun. Make money.) For me, that sums up many of my generalities of the Indian people.

I'm reminded of the time when I saw a news program about Wal-Mart opening stores in China to tap that country's vast consumer market. An American was being interviewed, and he was apparently a general manager in charge of overseeing many Chinese employees at a newly opened Wal-Mart store in China. During the interview, he said something to the effect:

> The people here work. I mean, these Chinese employees really work hard. And I never hear them say things like an American employee would, something like, "Boss, my daughter has a school soccer game at four o'clock tomorrow afternoon. Can I get off work early tomorrow so I can see her play?" Here, workers would never say such a thing. The work ethic here is incredible. During breaks, you don't see these Chinese employees laughing and joking around too much. They sip their tea and smoke their cigarettes. Then they get right back to work. They never complain. And they don't ask questions like, "Does this company offer a 401(k) plan or daycare services?"

For me, these observations of the work ethic of the Chinese people also apply to Indians. At Gitmo, I observed the migrant workers who were working for a subsidiary of Halliburton. These Gitmo migrant workers were essentially construction workers from the Philippines, Jamaica, India, or Pakistan. One couldn't help but notice that the Jamaicans were generally big, tall, and jovial. They often smiled and gave themselves high fives, and when they laughed, they laughed out loud. As to the Filipinos,

I never saw one who was taller than five-foot-eight. Some were skinny, but many were chubby. And, like the Jamaicans, these Filipinos were fun-loving types who joked around a lot. On weekends, I'd see them drinking beer and playing ping-pong. Then there were the Indian and Pakistani migrant workers. I couldn't tell them apart—physically, they looked the same. They were all thin, and most were short, too. And in contrast to the high-fiving Jamaicans and beer-drinking Filipinos, I never saw the Indian or Pakistani migrant workers laughing, smiling, or joking around during their breaks from work. I never saw any of them drink beer either at the few Gitmo bars. And unlike the Jamaicans who would say, "Hello, maauunn," when you walked by them, the Indian and Pakistani migrant workers never spoke a word to us American soldiers.

In short, the Indian and Pakistani migrant workers were serious. There was no joking around, no smiles, no greetings, and no beer on weekends. They worked, and they didn't joke around like the Jamaicans and Filipinos.

I found the movie *Trying to Find Humor in the Muslim World* on point on this very subject. The main character goes to India to find humor.[3] His mission failed because there's not much humor in India and it's not just the Muslim Indians—I think the same could be said of Hindu Indians who comprise the overwhelming bulk of the population. Humor is just not in the culture. Nor is having fun, at least how we in the West define it. Drinking beer and going clubbing doesn't happen in India. And concepts like comedians and comedy clubs are foreign to Indians.

There are a few rebuttals to this observation/generality of mine, rebuttals to this notion of Indians being a serious people. Indians do go out and watch movies, so that's one aspect of having fun.[4] And they also have one huge spectator sport, cricket. But these exceptions aside, Indians are very serious people and have an incredible work ethic. But why are they serious? I speculate that, for Indians, a big part of life is getting ahead, and central to getting ahead in life is making money. It's all about acquiring wealth.

If you ask a Westerner about the meaning of life, one will often hear:

---

3   India is the second-largest Muslim country in the world, second only to Indonesia.

4   Bollywood produces more movies than Hollywood.

- ♦ To be a good person
- ♦ To leave this earth in better shape than how I found it
- ♦ To do good work

At times, there would be a Christian perspective to such a question. "Well, the meaning of life is to believe in Christ so I'll be saved and make it to heaven."

Such would be some of the responses of Westerners, but I think that, if the question were asked to an Indian, one would hear, "The meaning of life? The meaning of life is how much money you have in your wallet. Life is about making money to have nice things and take care of my family."

True, within Hinduism, there are these leaders and even gurus who preach about the importance of spirituality and "being in one with the universe." Such messages, in part, run in contrast to wealth accumulation and materialism, but Latika and her sisters tell me that there's a high degree of fraud with these leaders, priests, and gurus preaching spirituality.

"Some are cheats, Paul," Latika once told me. "These gurus dressed in robes claiming spiritual knowledge, they're cheats. In the end, they want money. They especially want Americans and Europeans to visit their groups in India, but they always ask for money because that's what they're after."

Such a comment from my wife reminds me of certain parts of *Slumdog Millionaire*. After watching the movie with Latika, I couldn't help myself for I had tons of questions for her. Here are a couple:

Are there really kids like that in India? Dirt poor kids left on the street to live on their own?	Yes.
Are the divisions between Hindus and Muslims that great? Do Hindus sometimes attack Muslims and drive them out of their neighborhoods?	Yes, sometimes.

Are there street thugs who lure and/or kidnap homeless street kids, drug them up, and pour acid in their eyes so they become permanently blind and permanent beggars?"	Unfortunately, some Indian crooks do. It's a fraud. Many Indians will do anything for money. There are crooks who even kidnap people, drug them, and remove one of their victim's kidneys so they can sell the kidney on the black market for money. It's all about money.

So money and the accumulation of wealth factor greatly for many Indians. True, India has one of the fastest-growing economies in the world. It also boasts excellent schools. It produces great software engineers and medical doctors. It is a nuclear power. The list can go on. But on the flip side of that coin is poverty. An entire half of India's population lives in poverty. In my opinion, that plays into the serious people and wealth accumulation argument. Moreover, the need for money and wealth accumulation is not just found among the ranks of India's poor. Well-to-do Indians are also into wealth accumulation or more wealth accumulation. I attribute this money issue to an incredible work ethic, perhaps tradition, the obligation of taking care of one's family, and the status and image that comes with money and wealth.

Another observation—in general, Indians are not good tippers. Unlike in the United States, in India, people don't tip service people. There is no tradition of tipping in India. Me, I'm a good tipper, while Latika, she rarely tips. And one last observation: I've known Indian professionals—doctors, software engineers, and the like—who, even though they have high-paying jobs, also own convenience stores and other side businesses. I once painted the home of an Indian diplomat who was part-owner of a car wash business. Why would a medical doctor own a convenience store? Why would a diplomat own a car wash business? It's all about the money.

Indian expatriates

Many Indians leave India for better economic opportunities in America, Europe, Asia, and the Middle East. I'll further describe this expatriate phenomena later.

Latika has six siblings, and of the seven children in her family, five came to the United States on foreign student visas. All of these five siblings, my wife included, pursued higher education here in the states.

My father-in-law, Mr. Sreenivasulu, lived and worked outside of India for most of his life, and his family, for the most part, weren't with him while he was working overseas in places like Bahrain, the United Arab Emirates, Japan, even Africa. In a typical year, my father-in-law would visit his family once, maybe twice, in Chennai (Madras) India. Latika has told me his visits would last from seven to ten days.

I think my wife's family story is a typical Indian one with the father leaving India to better provide for his family, and his children pursuing higher education in the United States. Money . . . a better life . . . accumulating wealth . . . a serious people . . . not too many laughs . . . no drinking beer . . . no dancing. That is a typical Indian story.

The many nations within India

When I studied international relations, I learned about the concept of a nation. Essentially, a nation is a group of people having their own distinct culture, and central to culture are things such as language, religion, dress, cuisine, music, or even the physical characteristics or ethnicity of people. The concept of a nation wasn't too hard for me to grasp because Quebec had actually been used as an example of a nation in a class I once took.

"Canada is a binational country," the professor told us. "There are two nations in Canada, English Canada and French Canada, with the latter being mostly Quebecers in the province of Quebec."

The concept was easy for me to grasp because, coming from northern Maine and being a descendent of French Canadians myself, I got it. A nation. Own language, own religion, or own food, music, and so forth.

Of course, back then, a perfect example of a country having more than one nation was the then Soviet Union. Prior to its breakup, the Soviet Union had sixteen big subdivisions called republics. I think it's fair to say each one of those republics was a nation. Places like the Ukraine or Georgia, those were nations. The fact is Ukrainians have their own distinct culture. Today, after the breakup of the Soviet Union, it's its own country. So is Georgia.

India, like the former Soviet Union, is a country with many nations. I once read that India within itself is really "A United Nations of its own."

Moreover, it's sometimes argued that India itself is a British creation because prior to British colonial rule, there was no India—it was different regions ruled by different monarchs, and these different regions had their own language and culture. They were separate nations.

That's still true today for India has many nations within it. It amazes me how Latika can look at an Indian here in the United States and tell with fairly good accuracy where that Indian is originally from or where his parents are from. The big giveaway is one's surname. India has many languages, and its twenty-eight states are in some ways linguistically based. If you give my wife an Indian surname, she can tell you a lot about that person.

"Gupta," I once asked. I wanted to test her knowledge of surnames and Indian states.

"Oh, Gupta. Guptas are from the north, usually Delhi."

"What about the Bengali language?"

"No doubt about it. People speaking Bengali are from the state of West Bengal."[5]

"What about the name Mookencheril Cherian Joseph?"

"Absolutely no doubt about it. This is a person from the state of Kerala. People from the state of Kerala speak Malyalam."

I could tell Latika was dead-on. She was three for three. She hadn't missed a question.

"What about your own surname, Sreenivasulu?"

"With a name like ours, Sreenivasulu, anything ending in 'julu' or 'sulu,' people in India can tell right away that we are from the state of Andhra Pradesh." Latika then told me that, in India, one gets his surname from his father's first name. "My father's first name is Sreenivasulu. That is why our last name is Sreenivasulu."

"That's interesting. Honey, I like the Indian-American writer, D'Nesh D'Souza. Where's Mr. D'Souza from?"

"Easy. D'Souza is a Portuguese name. He's from the state of Goa. The Portuguese conquered Goa and made it a colony. They converted the people to Christianity. I'm pretty sure Mr. D'Souza is a Christian."[6]

"What about the surname Ramachandran?"

---

[5]   Incidentally, in *The Namesake*, the Indians moving to the United States are Bengalis.

[6]   In fact, D'Souza's family is from Goa, and they are Christians.

21

Immediately, Latika told me that such a name is definitely of the Brahmin caste and from the state of Tamil Nadu. She was right again. One's surname in India often indicates the state or region he is from and the caste he belongs to. And region and especially caste form the basis of one's loyalty.

India's caste system

The caste system in India is a very complicated subject. It's also fluid and adapting more and more. There are castes. Then there are castes within castes, but, in general, it's recognized that there are four castes. They are:

Brahmins	The Brahmins are the highest caste in the social order of India. Way back in history, they were essentially the religious teachers. The Brahmins and only the Brahmins knew and read the Sanskrit language. Hinduism, an old religion indeed, recognized the caste system and reaffirmed the Brahmins as leaders.
Ksatriyas	This is the second-highest caste, and Latika's family belongs to this caste. Historically, this caste consisted of the warriors and the nobility. Government and political jobs also went to the Ksatriyas.
Vaisyas	Traders, merchants, and skilled workers made up this caste.
Sudras	These were the untouchables, the lowest caste. Back in history, they were also the slaves.

Some of this stuff (the regionalism of India and its caste system) is hard for an American to grasp, yet alone swallow and accept. My last name is Bouchard. Once in a while, I'll hear a comment like, "Mr. Bouchard, with a name like that, you gotta be from Louisiana."

There's some logic there for Bouchard is a French name and Louisiana was a former French colony. The name Bouchard is very common in Quebec, but it can also be a Cajun name as well. Still, I've met Bouchards from many states: the New England states, Florida, Virginia, Colorado, New Mexico, and so forth. America is a transient society. People move around a lot namely because of job demands, but also because of things like climate, interest, and curiosity. The phenomenon of the melting pot is very real in America, and I think it's one of our strengths.

Some examples come to mind. When my National Guard unit was at Gitmo, our squad was getting a brief lesson from an Army soldier who happened to be a blonde-haired, blue-eyed girl from California. One of our squad members, a Hispanic, remarked on her nametag.

"Sergeant, I see your nametag says Hernandez. I'm just curious. Do you speak Spanish?"

"No," she said. "My husband, who's also in the Army, is from Puerto Rico. I took his last name. I don't speak a word of Spanish."

Here in America, people move around, and they marry who they want to marry. It's all part of the American experience. Sure there's regionalism here and there—the South, New England, the Midwest, and the Pacific Northwest. Yes, Jews are encouraged to marry Jews, and Mormons tend to marry Mormons. Also, there are family pressures and parental expectations here in the United States, but it's nothing like the rigid social structures brought about by the many languages, regions, and castes found in India.

My wife and her family are of the Ksatriya caste, but they lived in a Brahmin section of Madras. Latika told me that, when she was growing up, her Brahmin neighbors rarely, if ever, spoke to her and her family members.

"And forget being invited to a house owned by Brahmins. Brahmins would never invite someone of another caste into their home unless it was absolutely necessary. Even for a Brahmin to touch someone of another caste is taboo. Not even a handshake. The Brahmins never acknowledged us. They knew we were not part of their caste."

Current forces in India are working to change the caste system, but, as is often the case, change can sometimes take awhile.

Emigration and the Indian brain drain

Many Indians leave India in search of better economic opportunities elsewhere. For unskilled laborers, the Indian emigration phenomena is quite straightforward.

Better wages are overseas, so that's where I'll go to work.

A lot of these laborers end up in Middle Eastern countries, and they send substantial portions of their wages back home to support their families. For skilled Indians, however, the emigration story is a bit more complicated because one's caste comes into play.

In the late 1980s, when I was in graduate school in Washington DC, I noticed that many convenience stores were owned and operated by Indians and many taxicab drivers were also Indians. And the same could be said of hotels—I noticed many Indian immigrants getting into the hotel business, especially in South Florida where my parents spent winters. Additionally, one couldn't help but notice that a good number of doctors and university professors in the United States, especially in the sciences, were Indians. Some fifteen years later, when I met Latika, I inquired about this Indian immigration experience.

"The merchant class, the Indians owning convenience stores and hotels, they tend to be from northern India. In the south, education is more emphasized, and that's where a lot of the doctors and software engineers come from. The way things are run in India, the opportunities sometimes just aren't there."

"What do you mean?'"

"There's a lot of reverse discrimination in India."

Indeed, in India, the system heavily favors and gives breaks to the lower castes, and I later learned this favoritism of the lower castes is especially true in public sector jobs and higher learning, like admissions into graduate schools or medical schools.

For example, when an Indian applies for school or any type of public sector job, he must list his caste. Tests and entrance exams are also often given, but the score one must achieve on those tests to get into the particular school or get the job itself depends on one's score and caste. I was awestruck to learn how these important cutoff scores vary greatly among castes.

Take, for example, my sister-in-law, Prema. Prema blazed the emigration trail for her family because she was the first family member to immigrate to the United States. Prema came to the United States on a foreign student visa, but she told me her original plan was to go to medical school in India.

"I scored a ninety on the entrance exam, but, because of my caste, I needed to score a ninety-five. For Brahmins, they need to score something like a ninety-eight. The lower castes get into medical schools with scores in the seventies."

This favoritism of the lower castes was further explained to me in law school when I took a course called comparative constitutional law where I in part learned about the Indian Constitution. What follows are a few articles from that constitution, articles that specifically outline favoritism and set-asides for the lower castes.[7]

Article 16(4)	Nothing in this article shall prevent the state from making any provision for the reservation of appointments or posts in favor of any backward class of citizens, which, in the opinion of the state, is not adequately represented in the services of the state.
Article 46	This article is entitled "Promotion of Educational and Economic Interests of Scheduled Castes, Scheduled Tribes, and Other Weaker Sections."
Article 330	This article is entitled "Reservation of Seats for Scheduled Castes and Scheduled Tribes in the House of the People." It specifically states legislative seats will be assigned according to caste. Seats shall be reserved in the House of the People for the scheduled castes and scheduled tribes.

In *Imagining India: The Idea of a Renewed Nation*, successful software entrepreneur Nandan Nilekani mentions these educational and job set-asides for the lower castes, and he also writes about India's political system where voters vote for caste in exchange for certain public goods including government jobs. He writes that patronage is the key to buying votes, and he further argues India needs to do away with such loyalties, set-asides, and outright corruption of the public sector. In the end, he advocates for a more fair and efficient private sector model where jobs are awarded because of merit.

---

[7] The lower castes are sometimes referred to as the "backward class" or the "scheduled castes" or "the untouchables."

The way I see it, India's emigration issue is in part affected by demand-pull forces. There are better-paying jobs outside of India, and this attracts Indian labor. But, as I learned from Latika and her family, there are also supply-push forces at work because those of the higher castes are essentially pushed out of India since a substantial number of jobs and educational opportunities are reserved for lower castes, lower castes that historically were discriminated against.

India and education

India is a land of contrasts. It generates wealth and has a number of billionaires, yet half of its population lives in poverty. It's a world leader in software engineering and networking, yet many of its roads and highways are in dire need of repair. And when one looks at the topic of education in India, that is also not immune to contrasts because India has top-notch schools producing some of the best doctors, scientists, and professors, but it has the largest number of school dropouts in the world, and many of its citizens are illiterate.

"Many Indians want to pursue education, but there are only so many slots available in Indian schools," Latika once told me when I inquired about how she came to the United States to study. "Because of the limited seats available and set-asides for lower castes, many of us compete for foreign student visas."

She told me that competition, that is, the competition to get a foreign student visa to get into an American, Canadian, Australian, or European university, is very competitive indeed.

"My family was lucky in that there is an American consulate office in Madras. That's where you get the foreign student visa. First, you have to apply to the university overseas and get accepted on the condition you receive a foreign student visa. You have to make sure you have the right GRE scores, GMAT scores, and TOEFL[8] scores, everything you need to be accepted into the programs."

Latika then said one's finances have to be in order as well, whether it's financial aid or a scholarship or teacher assistance program. Once all of that is taken care of, the next step is getting the foreign student visa itself.

---

[8] Test of English as a Foreign Language

"The lines are incredible," Latika told me, referring to her experiences of getting a foreign student visa. "The consulate may open at nine o'clock, but the line outside can start at two o'clock in the morning. I know of some people who actually pay strangers and street people to take up a spot in line. That way, the true aspiring student can show up at eight o'clock, see where his paid person is in line, and take his spot. It prevents you from having to wake up at one o'clock in the morning to get in line at two o'clock."

The foreign student visa application sometimes requires an interview, and it sometimes doesn't.

"I'm glad I got mine when I did," Latika once told me. "After September 11, it's been harder to get a foreign student visa."

I've known a few Indians who pursued their educations here in the United States, particularly Latika and her sisters, but others as well. By observing how these Indian students went about pursuing their degrees, I once again witnessed the themes and generalities previously mentioned:

- Indians are a serious people with a strong work ethic.
- India is not a car nation.
- India does not have a beer-drinking culture.
- Indians, in general, do not have pets.
- Indians study hard.

That's how I'd sum up the Indian educational experience in the United States because the Indians I've known who've pursued higher education here were all extremely hardworking and dedicated. And, importantly, what they didn't do or engage in was very telling.

For example, never have I seen an Indian student join a fraternity or sorority. Also, so few of the Indians I knew in college and graduate school had cars—indeed, they walked to school and classes. Moreover, never have I seen an Indian drink beer or date, and so rarely would I see an Indian attend a collegiate sporting event. Finally, there were no pets either. Indians do not have pets.

Hit the books. See the occasional movie. Watch the occasional cricket match on TV. But that's about it as far as entertainment goes. Indians studying abroad is not about fraternities, sororities, dating, drinking beer, or otherwise having fun. It's about studying and hopefully getting a good-paying job.

Superstition

Little statues of Buddha[9] strategically placed in rooms; even more brass statues of Ganesha, the elephant-headed Hindu god of new beginnings; and still more miniature remnants of elephants also placed in rooms.

That, in part, is how our home is decorated because Latika, like many Indians, believes Buddha, Ganesha, and elephants are all positive symbols. She also believes, again like many Indians, that statues of elephants bring good luck.

When Latika and I bought our home, she made sure the front of our home faced north. And once bought, she made sure to stock our home's various rooms with tiny statues of Ganesha, Buddha, and elephants. If you check out Indian restaurants, you'll also find small statues of Buddha, elephants, and especially Ganesha. Latika tells me this is all about positive energy driving out negative energy and bringing good luck.

Then there's the topic of astrology, yet another example of the superstitious nature of Indians. Indians are big believers in astrology. They make sure the stars are lining up properly for the right events to occur.

"In India," Latika once told me, "we have many astrologers. They generally do good business." She explained that the customers of these numerous astrologers might include:

+ Students waiting for exam results and wondering how they fared
+ Fathers inquiring if a particular man is suitable for marrying his daughter
+ Elderly people wondering if they'll succumb to cancer

Here in the United States, we believe seven is a lucky number and thirteen is an unlucky one. We have our own superstitions, but it's paltry compared to the breadth and depth of the superstitious beliefs of Indians. In fact, Latika tells me Indians will often reserve commentary on any future event for fear that simply talking about something that hasn't happened yet will influence its outcome.

---

9   Buddha, incidentally, was a former Hindu who criticized the caste system.

Love of gold and jewelry

Indians, to include Indian men, love gold and jewelry. If you check out Little Indias in major American cities like Jackson Heights in Queens or Devon Street in Chicago, you'll inevitably find Indian restaurants, shops selling saris, and, undoubtedly, jewelry stores. Indian women love wearing tons of bangles on their wrists, and Indian men love gold watches. Moreover, it's common practice at Indian weddings for the bride's family to give gold to the groom.

On occasion, I tease Latika about this gold-giving, reminding her family failed protocol by not honoring Indian traditions, that is, by not giving me any gold at our wedding.

"The gold is mine, Paul," Latika told me. "My money is my money; your money is my money, too."

Cuisine

Ever since I dated and then eventually married Latika, I've developed a fondness for Indian cuisine, so much so that it now ranks right up there with my favorite American and Italian dishes.

Like many Indians, Latika doesn't eat beef or pork. Some Indians eat lamb, but she doesn't. Latika tells me there are many different types of regional cuisines and dishes in India, but the two primary distinctions are North Indian cuisine versus South Indian cuisine, with South Indian cuisine being, at times, entirely vegetarian.

Our favorite Indian restaurant in El Paso is called Chutney.[10] Its menu is quite extensive. Here are a few examples:

Soups	
Mulligatawny	This soup is made of vegetable or chicken broth with lentils and spices. It's my favorite soup.
Rasom	This is a traditional South Indian sour and spicy soup. It's way too hot and spicy for me, but Latika eats it with no problem.

---

[10] Chutney is a spicy condiment made chiefly from mangos.

Appetizers	
Samosas	Samosas are potato and peas stuffed in crispy wheat bread and deep fried. They're the most common type of appetizer in Indian cuisine.
Bhel poori	This is puffed rice, tossed with onion, chili, tomato, cilantro, and chutney.
Cutlet	This dish is a mixed vegetable patty with spices.
Samosa chat	These are samosas mixed with a bean sauce. It's very good.
Lamb shish kebab	This is specially marinated minced lamb on skewers.

Main Dishes	
Dosas	South Indian restaurants will often offer dosas as a main dish. Dosas are thin and crispy rice crepes, often filled with onions and potatoes. The crepe is huge, a meal onto itself. It is folded in half and covers an entire plate. Just the center portion of the fold has the potatoes and onions. Latika tells me many South Indians have dosas for breakfast, but these breakfast dosas aren't as large as the main dish dosas.
Idli-Vada combo	These are steamed rice muffins and fried lentil donuts served with sambar (lentil-based sauce) and chutney.
Channa masala	These are chickpeas cooked in exotic spices.
Veg korma	These are fresh vegetables cooked with onion and a coconut-based sauce.
Chicken tikka masala	This is my favorite Indian dish. It's boneless chicken cooked in a creamy tomato sauce.
Chicken curry	Probably the most popular of all Indian dishes, this is chicken in a homemade, authentic Southern sauce.

Chicken biryani	This is Latika's favorite. It's chicken and basmati rice cooked with spices. I like the dish as well, but I always have to tell the waiter, "Make it mild, please."
Tandoori chicken	One of the most popular dishes in Indian cuisine, this dish is chicken marinated in yogurt and mild spices.
Indian Breads	There are so many different types of breads in Indian cuisine. Whether it's plain naan, garlic naan, tandoori roti, chappati, or onion kulcha, Indian breads are all delicious in my opinion. They're usually either soft flour bread or whole wheat soft bread, and they're always cooked in a clay oven.
Sweets and Desserts	Indian desserts are varied, but some of the most common are often comprised of cheese balls or round dough balls cooked in creamy milk and served with almonds and pistachios. Another dessert is mango custard, which is my favorite.
Beverages	India is famous for its tea. Their coffee is excellent as well. Chai, a sweetened tea, is very popular, too. Though India doesn't have a beer-drinking culture, many Indian restaurants, at least those in the United States, serve beer and wine, with Kingfisher and Taj Mahal being two popular beers. Then there's mango lassi, a sort of yogurt drink made from mangoes. It is my favorite Indian beverage.

ABCD

Latika and I often dine out at Chutney on Friday nights after work. On one such Friday night, I immediately noticed a woman working the tables. The sight struck me as odd because I had never noticed waitresses working at Chutney—only men worked the tables. Latika and I sat down, and the new waitress came to our table to take our order.

"Hi. How's everyone doing?" she said in unaccented English. She was a beautiful girl, and I guessed she was in her mid-twenties. "Can I offer you any drinks? Appetizers?" She handed us the menus.

"Water for me," Latika said.

"Mango lassi, please."

Then Latika said, "We're actually ready to order. I'll have the chicken birayani."

"Chicken tika masala, please."

"Great," said the waitress. "I'll bring your drinks right out." She picked up the menus, turned, and headed straight for the kitchen.

"Guess they hired a waitress this time," I told Latika.

She looked at me. "She's an ABCD."

My mind started racing. I was thinking of vocabulary letters.

"She's an ABCD. She's an American-Born Confused Desi."

I was still confused. I sort of got the American-born portion, but I wasn't grasping this "desi" term. I was thinking daisies, like the flowers.

"What the heck is that?" I asked, perplexed.

"It's a term we Indians have describing Indians who are born here in the United States. Oftentimes, they're confused. You know, like am I American or Indian?"

Latika and I had a long discussion that night about ABCDs. As we ate our chicken biryani and chicken tikka masala, I learned that Indians are referred to as "desis." That was new to me because I had never heard the term. During dinner, Latika made her arguments as to how the term came about and why ABCD rings true while I argued the opposite—there was no confusion on the new waitress' part; she was American, born and raised.

"It doesn't matter where your parents are from. Once one is in the United States, he'll adopt American ways and culture," I said. "Bobby Jindal speaks English like an American with all the slang and stuff," I argued. "And I bet that, when he was growing up and playing sports, he played baseball, football, and basketball, not cricket."

As to the main character in the movie *Bend It Like Beckham*, I said the United Kingdom has a similar phenomenon to what we have here in the United States, the melting pot. "Yes, the girl in the movie was getting pressures from her traditional Indian parents, but she'll be British soon enough."

At one point in the conversation, I shifted gears and focused on Chutney's new hire.

"Notice how the waitress asked how everyone was doing? Drinks? Appetizers? The Indian-born waiters here never talk like that. They aren't as friendly and informal. Good for Chutney. 'Bout time they hire a waitress. ABCD it is."

It was a good and lively talk with Latika, and the mango lassi and chicken tikka masala were excellent as always.

Applying the problem of the Russian soul to Indians

In 2008, my particular job in the Army JAG Corps involved traveling to San Diego on occasion. Sometimes there were direct flights from El Paso to San Diego, but, more often than not, my flight itinerary involved stops at the large airport in Phoenix.

One time, when I had a long wait for a connecting flight out of Phoenix, I bought a copy of both the *New York Times* and *Wall Street Journal.* In one of those two newspapers, I read a short piece by a Russian-born American writer who lived in New York City. In her article, the writer argued that the problem with Russians is the Russian soul, for the Russian soul is a soul that derives pleasure out of seeing other people in misery. That's some pretty harsh stuff and in no way a compliment.

What type of people derives pleasure and happiness out of seeing others in misery? Not a nice quality indeed. Does this problem of the Russian soul apply to Indians?

It made me think of a few things Latika and I had previously discussed:

"In India, sometimes, even within families, a family member rejoices when another family member's visa is rejected." Latika further told me that the rejoicing is not based on the thinking, "Oh good, you're not going to America or the United Kingdom. That is good because I love you and I don't want to see you leave."

Latika said, "The family member is actually happy his sibling or friend was not successful in getting the visa because India is a very competitive country. In India, if you see someone succeed, some Indians think this means there's less of a chance they themselves will succeed. It's jealousy, and it's also about competition and superstitions."

Is this jealousy part of the Indian soul? Do Indians, in general, see things as a zero-sum game? No win-win? If you win, then that means I lose?

Take *Slumdog Millionaire*, a movie that, in my opinion, was very well done and deserving of its many awards. After watching the movie with Latika, I naturally had many questions because, on many levels, things depicted in the movie were hard for a Westerner to swallow.

"Are there really thugs in India who kidnap street kids, tie them up, pour acid in their eyes so the kids become permanently blind, and then use these blind kids as beggars to raise money for the thugs?"

"Yes."

"And what about the host of the millionaire show in the movie? Boy, did I get bad vibes from him. And the audience. I hated the audience, especially in the beginning of the movie."

In the movie, the host of the show actually goes out of his way to ridicule and debase the poor contestant, the one from the slums who is answering the questions correctly. And when the host makes fun of the contestant, the audience laughs along with the host.

What the hell is this? The host and the audience are actually rooting against the contestant.

Luckily, the tide changes toward the end of the movie when the audience finally comes to its senses and roots for the poor contestant, but the evil host never roots for the contestant. He even has the audacity during a break to slip an answer to the contestant, an answer to a question that's worth a lot of money. The slipped answer, without surprise, is incorrect. It's knowingly and deliberately incorrect by the host, a host who is doing his best to trip up the contestant and have him lose.

I gave a big thumbs-up during the scene where the contestant, following his hunch, figures the host is working against him. That's when the contestant gives the other available answer, not the answer the evil, conniving host had slipped to him during a bathroom break.

A show's host working against a contestant and an audience laughing at the host's rude jokes directed at the contestant—what the hell is this? In America, if a show's host made fun of the contestant and worked to ensure the contestant's failure, there undoubtedly would be lawsuits, and the topic would dominate the news and radio talk shows.

- The contestant or his family would sue the program for unfair practices, general unfairness, and discrimination, the whole gamut. They'd find a basis for a lawsuit, and certain lawyers would line up and gladly take the case and its cause.
- Callers would call in and demand the resignation of the host. "Fire his ass" would be their motto. "I'm ashamed such a thing could take place in America," wouldn't be far-fetched and unheard of.
- There would be letters to the editor written on the topic, protesting as to how a host could actually go out of his way to make a contestant lose.
- There would be pressure on the boards of directors of the companies sponsoring the show, which would include:

  - The demand to fire the host
  - A formal apology by the company for such unconscionable behavior
  - Threats of banning the products of the corporations who are sponsors/advertisers of the show

That's what would happen in America if a host and an audience behaved liked what was depicted in *Slumdog* Millionaire—lawsuits, demands for resignations, and consumer boycotts. And there would also be a call for better audience participants, those who actually root for the contestant to win.

Importantly, I understand the need for movies to add drama because drama sells and movies need to sell something in order to bring in the revenues and be a hit. Hollywood does that, and I certainly don't think all the movies coming out of Hollywood are reflective and representative of American culture. In fact, I believe some American movies are not representative of America at all.

But what of Bollywood?[11] What about all those Indian movies? Are Indian movies representative of India? More to the point, was *Slumdog Millionaire* representative of India?

According to my wife, the answer is, sadly, yes.

---

[11] India, incidentally, makes more movies than any other country in the world.

Does the problem of the Russian soul apply to Indians? Do Indians, in general, derive pleasure from seeing others in misery, from seeing others lose? "I don't know" is the honest answer. One thing I do know (and this again comes from Latika) is that Indians, as Hindus and like Buddhists, believe in karma and destiny. When you believe in destiny, it's sort of an acknowledgement that you cannot affect what is happening to you. It's your destiny. It's also another way of saying things are the way they are and we can't change it. That it is what it is. Things are what they are.

From discussions with Latika, I've learned the karma argument carries some weight. Compassion for the poor? Compassion is really not a strong feeling among Indians, even financially well-off Indians. Give to charity? It's the same answer. Charitable giving is not too big among Indians. Things are the way they are. The poor are poor.

Then there's also this belief in reincarnation among Indians, and this also plays into the karma/destiny argument. *One is poor. That means he may have done something wrong in an earlier life. Now his punishment is to be poor and/or suffer in his current life.* Latika has told me that many Indians think this way.

In the end, I have many good things to say about India and its people, but the jealousy/overcompetitiveness/zero-sum mentality isn't one of them. The karma argument can sometimes bring some disastrous results as well. I say fire the host of *Slumdog Millionaire* and sue him. And give me the smiling Regis Philbin who actually wants the contestant to win. That's my final answer.

CHAPTER THREE

How Indians Normally Get Married

Marriages in India are mostly arranged marriages where it's mandatory for the parents to approve of the spouse of their son or daughter who is of marrying age. Arranged marriages are also popular for Indians living in the United States. Here's how marriage classifieds are typically done in India:

- ◆ Vaishnav, Vanik family invites proposals for their American citizen daughter, twenty-five years old, five-foot-three, good-looking. BS in applied psychology and human relations, has good job. Alliance sought from smart, professionally qualified boys hailing from Vaishnov, Vanik/Gujarati families. Write to . . .
- ◆ Muslim girl, twenty-three, software development engineer, belongs to financially sound family. Parents seek suitable, professional Muslim boy. Write . . .
- ◆ Telegu, Baliju, Naidu parents seek for MD daughter, twenty-five, five-foot-five, very fair, beautiful, American-raised, first-year residency. Groom should be American-raised, MD, nonsmoker, Hindu Telegu. Write to . . .
- ◆ Bride, born 1983, five-foot-one, slim, fair, medical line, lives in New York. Looking for Punjabi professional boy holding H-1B visa or United States citizen. Reply to . . .
- ◆ NI Hindu specialist, United States MD, forty, five-foot-eleven, very fair, earning seven figures, seeks pretty wife with family values. MD/Law, thirty-one to thirty-five, tristate (Connecticut-New York-New Jersey) area. E-mail . . .
- ◆ Hindu, forty-two, self-employed, home owner. Divorcée ok. Caste no bar. Call . . .

Most of these ads are from an old *India Abroad* issue. *India Abroad*, an Indian-produced, American-based newspaper, provides news about India to Indians living in the United States and Canada. The newspaper has editions for Chicago, Dallas, Los Angeles, New York/New Jersey/ Connecticut, and Toronto. The other ads are from an old edition of the *India Tribune*, New York edition. *India Tribune* is similar to *India Abroad*.

Placing such an ad in such a newspaper is generally the first step for Indian parents if they're looking for a suitable mate for their son or daughter. Before I get to the other steps, let's analyze some of these ads:

- The first ad kicks off with Vaishnav and mentions the Vanik family. Vaishnav and Vanik are subcastes of the Brahmin caste. The caste system is quite complicated, and I only scratched the surface earlier when I mentioned the four basic castes. However, an Indian reading the words *Vaishnav*, *Vanik*, and *Gujarati* would know what the words mean and what the person who paid for the ad was looking for. Gujarati is a language. In this case, it means the parents are from the state of Gujarat.
- The third ad starts with Telegu and then reads, "Baliju, Naidu parents." Telegu is a language.[12] Naidu is a subcaste, and Baliju is a subcaste of Naidu.

Caste, subcaste, language, religion, and state, all of these things matter when finding a suitable mate for an Indian marriage. And Indian Muslims also have arranged marriages, as exemplified by the second ad that mentions the availability of a Muslim woman.[13] Finally, also notice how profession, salary, income, degrees, and skin tone factor into these ads. Latika said these factors are also crucial for finding the right mate.

"Many ads will indicate where the person got their degree from. A lot of them will say 'Ivy League-educated.' This means a lot to Indians. It boils down to status, which is important."

So not only does the educational degree factor in, but also where that degree was obtained.

---

[12] It's actually the language that my wife and her family speak.

[13] India is the second-largest Muslim country in the world behind Indonesia.

Notice the mention of American citizenship, American-raised, and H-1B visa. For Indian parents, such designations are coveted because this means the person is a citizen of America or can at least work in America, which is huge.

Also, notice how often skin tone is mentioned. Looking over the ads, I noticed there were only two tones that seem to be mentioned: fair and wheatish.

"Skin tone matters to Indians," Latika told me.

Hooking up Indian-style is sure different than how it's done here in America.

Then I really thought about it. There are differences all right, but there are similarities as well. Obviously, we don't have the caste system in America, and the thought of one having to marry someone from a particular state in the United States is absolutely not applicable. But let's face it—race, religion, and profession factor into the topic of marriage. Just look at dating ads in American newspapers and online sites:

- Divorced, white Christian woman seeking nonsmoking Christian man . . .
- Single, black woman looking for a black man to . . .
- Successful professional looking for professional woman age thirty-two to thirty-nine for . . .
- Nonsmoking professional woman seeking professional man for companionship. I enjoy modern art, classical music, and long walks on beaches. Prefer nonsmoker who . . .

Such ads are the norm here in America, and race, religion, and profession factor in. Also consider Jews, Catholics, and Mormons—depending on the person and/or the family, there could be pressure to marry his own kind.

Still, the differences between Indians and Americans on the topic of hooking up are numerous. The Indian ads mention height and weight, but the American ads aren't as descriptive on that topic. Hair color for American woman is an issue (brunette, blonde, redhead), but Indian women are homogeneous on that subject—they overwhelmingly have black hair. Also, forget Indian ads exploring the issue of sexual orientation because homosexuality and bisexuality are taboo.

Finally, consider the biggest difference of all. The Indian ads are about marriage proposals while the American ads are about companionship. Marriage for Americans might come later. For Indians, they get right to tying the knot.

Let me end with one similarity, probably best described as a trend. Notice some of the Indian ads state "divorcée" or "caste no bar." Ten years ago, one wouldn't see those words in such ads, but India is liberalizing, that is, becoming more like Western countries such as the United States. Latika said the Indian divorce rate is still very low, although it's climbing. Where divorced Indians, especially divorced Indian women, would previously never have someone interested in them for marriage, now, with India liberalizing, there's a chance a divorced Indian woman can remarry.

The following is the Indian marriage process:

♦ The first step is often an ad in a newspaper, but another way of hooking up is when the prospective future bride and groom live close to one another and somehow know each other from school or social gatherings. If the families of the two marital prospects live close to one another, then the parents simply get together and gather information on the prospective bride and groom.

♦ Next is sending a picture and biography of the prospective bride or groom, including the all-important birthday and time of birth of the prospect.

♦ Then it's a visit to a local astrologer who has the important task of discovering if the prospective bride and groom are compatible, given their respective birthdays and times of birth.

♦ If there is compatibility, then the prospective groom meets the parents of the bride. It is important that the groom's parents (and sometimes his relatives) are part of this visit as well. Tea is served; questions and answers are exchanged. The groom, toward the end of the meeting, meets the prospective bride.

♦ If the parents agree a match is possible, then there is the discussion of the dowry. The prospective bride's family always gives the dowry, and both the bride and groom use it. A dowry can be money or a house or a car, and it often involves gold.[14]

---

[14] Historically, the groom's family always gave the dowry, but this changed decades ago.

◆ If everything is in order and all the parameters have been met, then there is another visit to an astrologer to select the most auspicious date for the wedding.

From what Latika told me, *The Namesake* accurately portrayed an arranged marriage. I liked *The Namesake* a lot—I thought it was an excellent movie—and if there's any theme to the movie, it's about the cultural differences between India and America.

For me, many scenes stick out in the movie, but the ones that most often come to mind are:

◆ The Indian-American college student brings his blonde American girlfriend to his home to meet his parents. His girlfriend keeps referring to his parents by their first names. That wouldn't be done in India. Latika tells me Indians don't refer to someone by his first or last name for they simply use the designation sir, ma'am, Mr., or Ms. This nonuse of names even applies to relatives, for a nephew or niece simply refers to his or her aunt or uncle as auntie or uncle. Moreover, the designation uncle or auntie can sometimes be used to refer to a senior person even if that person is not one's uncle or aunt. When the American girlfriend is first introduced to her Indian-American boyfriend's parents, she also shakes hands with his parents and kisses them on the cheek. Kissing on the cheek is not done in India.

◆ The Indian couple is walking together, and the wife mentions these cultural differences between the old country and her adoptive country, the United States. At one point, she turns to her husband, smiles, and says, "Shall we say like the Americans do, 'I love you?'" She says this in a joking and dismissive way.

In my opinion, the second scene is especially poignant because it shows that an arranged marriage isn't about romantic love. It's not about being interested in someone and falling in love with that someone. It's not about telling your wife or husband, "I love you." For such societies, marriage is about conserving and protecting social order, class, status, and perhaps even family wealth.

Truth be told, the concept of romantic love is relatively young in human history. It started in Europe, and as colonialism spread, so did the concept as well. But even in the early days of our nation's history, many marriages were arranged. Still to this day, many countries have arranged marriages or remnants of arranged marriages.

Latika and I did not have an arranged marriage. Ours was a Western-style courtship: date, get interested in one another, fall in love, and decide to marry. Still, I had to meet my in-laws, and that's the topic of the next chapter.

CHAPTER FOUR

Meeting the In-laws (Telephonically)

In March 2003, Latika and I went to South Florida to meet my parents. The visit went well. My parents are friendly and receptive, and they liked Latika. We were engaged at the time, but I didn't tell my parents that fact, not because I was ashamed of the engagement, but there were just so many potential questions with many of them having no definitive answers.

"Oh, you're getting married. When's the big date?"

"We don't know yet."

"How's law school going?"

"Good. Tough. Lots of classes left."

"When's your law school graduation?"

"I don't know. It depends on how many classes I'll take and pass during the summer session."

"Are you still thinking of practicing law in the Army? Why not work as a lawyer in a big law firm?"

"The big law firms hire the best students. I'm right at the fiftieth percentile of my class, but they want the top ten or twenty percent."

"Your wedding will be a Catholic wedding, right?"

"Well, that depends if the priest allows us to marry in the Catholic Church."

"Remember that your first marriage was not in the Church."

"Yes, I remember. It was not a Catholic wedding."

"See what happens when you don't get married in the Church."

"Yeah, yeah."

Essentially, I didn't want to deal with such potential questions. I grew up Catholic, and I'm still Catholic, but, if there's such a thing as a bad Catholic, I'm it. I'm fairly good about attending Mass, but fairly good means I'm not at Mass dutifully every Sunday. I don't regularly do the fish thing on Fridays, I hardly know any of the saints, and I really don't know and understand the Bible all that well either. Still, I'm not shopping around in search of another religion because I don't really consider myself all that religious. I pray, give to charities, and go to Mass somewhat regularly. That's about it.

So our visit to South Florida to meet my parents went well. I didn't mention the all-important engagement, but it went well. Besides, I think my parents had an inkling Latika and I were serious.

Now it was my turn to meet my future in-laws. It was the spring of 2003, shortly after Latika and I had visited my parents. I had recently started my third and final year in law school, and I was still worried about my law classes, whether I'd pass them all and graduate in December. I also dreaded the upcoming bar exam that, if all worked as planned, I'd be taking in a year in the spring of 2004. Finally, I also worried whether the Army JAG Corps would accept my application.

Those many worries aside, Latika and I decided to get engaged in the spring of 2003. Shortly thereafter, I brought her to see my parents. Now it was my turn to meet Mr. and Mrs. Sreenivasulu. Unfortunately, I didn't have the money to fly to India to visit my future in-laws,[15] so I had to meet them via the telephone.

We were in Latika's apartment, the student apartment she shared with two of her sisters, when this important phone call took place. Before Latika dialed the phone number to her parents in India, she gave me some preparatory reminders.

She said, "Speak loud and clear and slowly."

"Okay."

"My mother speaks very little English, so you'll be talking to my father mostly."

"Okay."

"Tell my father that being a lawyer is a good and important thing in the United States."

"What do you mean?"

"Being a lawyer in India is not a big thing. It's not a desired occupation like it is here. Here in the United States, it seems to carry some status."

"Ghandi was a lawyer, wasn't he?"

---

[15] Flight tickets to India typically run around $1,500 apiece.

"Ghandi was poor. He didn't have any status until he became a civil rights leader."

"Okay."

"Tell my father that being a lawyer in the Army is a good thing and that Army lawyers make good money."

"But I'm not sure if the Army will accept my application to the JAG Corps because—"

"Just tell him lawyers make good money in this country."

"But I haven't graduated from law school yet. And what if I don't pass the bar exam?"

"Just tell him you'll make good money."

"Okay."

Latika dialed the number. In no time, she was speaking Telegu, her native tongue which I don't understand. After no more than a minute, she handed me the phone receiver.

There was silence.

What the hell? Break the ice.

I cleared my throat. "Hello, Mr. Sreenivasulu."

"Hello, Mr. Paul!" His voice was very loud.

"Uh, Mr. Sreenivasulu, it is nice to hear your voice. I go to law school with your daughter, Prema, and that is how I met your daughter, Latika. I would—"

"Ah yes, Mr. Paul. When were you born?"

Hmm? Latika didn't prepare me for this.

I went ahead and told him my birthdate.

"Mr. Paul, what time of the day were you born?"

Boy, I'm glad my mother told me this a long time ago.

"Uh, I was born at exactly ten o'clock in the morning, sir."

"Ah, very good. Very good." Then there was silence. "My wife will say hello."

"Oh, okay. Very well, sir."

I heard the phone being handed off.

"Hello," said Latika's mother in a soft voice.

"Hello, Mrs. Sreenivasulu."

"Hello."

The phone connection is good.

"Hello, Mrs. Sreenivasulu."

"Hello."

Then I heard the phone being handed off.

"Ah yes, Mr. Paul, my wife speaks little English."

"Oh, that's okay. It was nice of Mrs. Sreenivasulu to say hello."

"Ah yes. Very good." Then there was silence for maybe five seconds. "Do lawyers in America make good money?"

"Yes, sir."

"Ah, very good. This is very good." Then there was some silence. "Well, Mr. Paul, I wish you and your family good blessings."

"Thank you, sir. Thank you, Mr. Sreenivasulu. And good health to you and Mrs. Sreenivasulu."

"Ah yes. Very good. Very good."

I handed the phone to Latika, who was smiling. She started speaking Telegu to her father. I was off the hook.

Some fifteen minutes later, after all the sisters had spoken to their parents over the phone, Latika and I discussed my phone conversation with her dad.

Latika asked, "Did he ask you how much money you make?"

"Not really. He asked if lawyers in America make good money."

Latika sighed. "Well, what did you tell him?"

"I told him yes. Lawyers in America make good money."

"Good. Did he ask you your birthdate and time of birth?"

"Yes, what's up with that?"

Latika and her sisters laughed.

"He will see an astrologer soon, probably today, to see if we're a good match."

"So the stars and planets have to line up?"

"Yes, sort of. This is serious, Paul."

"Yes. Yes, it is."

"Did you talk to my mom?"

"Yes. She said hello."

"My mom doesn't speak much English, but she understands it."

"That's a deadly combination."

Latika's sisters were laughing, but Latika was serious.

"Okay, anything else?"

There was silence.

"You know, your father referred to me as Mr. Paul. He always referred to me by my first name, but with Mister in front of it."

"Yes, well, in India, that's how it is. Our last name is Sreenivasulu because that is my father's first name. In India, surnames are often the first name of the father."

"For real?"

"Yes. So you were wrong in calling him Mr. Sreenivasulu because that's his first name. But it's okay. My father is used to Westerners."

That was how my first telephone call with my in-laws went. There would be other phone conversations with them, and they were always short and cordial with the topics almost exclusively revolving around education level, career prospects, salary, and how my parents were doing. These phone conversations were always between Latika's father and me, with him referring to me as Mr. Paul and me calling him Mr. Sreenivasulu.

Unfortunately, I never did hear about whether the stars and planets had lined up, but Latika told me not to worry.

"Besides, we're still getting married. It doesn't matter what some astrologer in Madras thinks or says."

Thanks to God, Jesus, all the saints, Ganesha, Vishnu, Buddha, karma, the stars and planets lining up, and so forth, the Army JAG Corps did accept my application in November 2003. The following month, I graduated from law school. My JAG application, however, was contingent upon me passing the bar exam.

In September 2003, I had signed up to take the New Mexico bar exam, which was slated to take place in late February 2004. After my law school graduation, I moved to Albuquerque and started studying. During that time, Latika and I decided to have our wedding in August of that year. If all worked as planned, I'd pass the bar in February, we would get married in August, and I'd start the Army JAG school in September. If I didn't pass the February bar, then I'd have another shot at it in July.

Thanks again to God, Jesus, all the saints, Ganesha, Vishnu, Buddha, karma, and so forth, I passed the New Mexico bar exam in February. August was the planned date for the wedding, and Latika and I had earlier decided we wanted both a Catholic and a Hindu wedding. The question then became, "Which wedding will we have first?"

Chapter Five

The Catholic Wedding

But I wasn't sure if I could have a Catholic wedding with Latika for the simple fact that Latika, as a Hindu, obviously wasn't a Catholic. I was under the impression that one had to be a Catholic to be married in the eyes of the Catholic Church. Plus I had struck out before. I wanted my first marriage/wedding to be a Catholic one, but a Catholic priest refused my then-fiancée because she wasn't Catholic. My response was that we'd get married in a Protestant chapel, which we did.

According to the Catholic theologian and writer, George Weigel, "We're all bad Catholics." At least I remember him saying that when I saw an interview of him on C-SPAN. If Mr. Weigel is correct, then, in my estimation, I'd classify myself as a really bad Catholic.

I don't consider myself all that religious. I go to Mass, pray, and give a bit to charity. That's it. I grew up Catholic. Where I'm from in northern Maine, it's all Catholic. Overall, I'm comfortable with the Church and its teachings. I must, however, admit I'm attracted to the Protestant concept of having a one-on-one relationship with God.

Anyway, I'm not shopping around for another religion. In 2004, I simply wanted both a Catholic and Hindu wedding for Latika and me. On the Catholic side, I had a backup plan if necessary. It was the same backup plan I had for my first marriage—if the Catholic Church wouldn't marry us, then I'd find a Protestant minister who would. The sticky point was that I believed, from what I heard from others, one must convert to Catholicism to be married in the Church. I knew Latika wouldn't convert, nor did I expect her to. In all likelihood, I really thought I'd have to exercise my backup plan of finding a Protestant minister to marry us.

When I lived in Albuquerque, I attended Mass at the Church of the Risen Savior Catholic Church. One weekday, I simply went to the church and asked to speak to a priest. In a few minutes, I was introduced to a burly, bearded, middle-aged priest. We sat down, and I got straight to the point.

"Father, my name's Paul. I'm Catholic. I'm also divorced. I'm currently engaged to a woman who is a Hindu. Father, I want our wedding to be a Catholic one."

"I see. And your first marriage? Was it in the Church?"

"No, Father. It was a Protestant ceremony."

"That's good," he said matter-of-factly. "In the eyes of God, that marriage doesn't count. If you were previously married in the Catholic Church, then you'd need an annulment."

"I see." I nodded my head.

The priest then asked me more questions about myself. He also wanted to meet Latika. I told him that could be arranged shortly. Then I mustered the gumption to ask him the key question.

"Does one have to be a Catholic to get married in the Church? Does one have to convert?"

"No," he said in a convincing way.

Still, I thought there was a strong preference for one to convert to Catholicism in order to be married in the Church.

"No, Paul," he continued, reassuring me some more. "One does not have to convert to Catholicism to be married in the Church. There is one requirement, however."

"I see." I braced myself for his answer.

"Should you and Latika have children, they should be baptized and raised in the Church."

"Yes, Father," I said.

I think Latika and I can live with that. Maybe. Yeah.

It was a hot Saturday in Albuquerque, August 20, 2004. For the previous two months, Latika, her sisters, and I had done all the preparations for both weddings—the right attire, reserving the receptions areas, sending out the wedding invitations, and so forth. It was a lot of work. On the Catholic side, the game plan was to get married at the Church of the Risen Savior and then have the reception at the Hyatt in downtown Albuquerque. For the Hindu wedding, we had rented space at a facility called Open Seed University, a plain building across the Rio Grande River in West Albuquerque where Eastern spiritualism classes were offered. The

Hindu wedding was slated for the next day, a Sunday. Truth be told, I insisted to Latika that the Catholic wedding be held first.

"If not, then there's the possibility our Catholic wedding will be declared void. If the Catholic priest somehow finds out we were married before the Catholic wedding, then it's possible he won't marry us."

What I told Latika was the truth, and she conceded. It's one of the few arguments I've ever won against her. Anyway, it was settled—the Catholic wedding would be on Saturday, August 20; the Hindu wedding would be on the very next day, Sunday, August 21.

*　*　*

I left my Albuquerque apartment in good time to pick up my parents, who were staying at a nearby hotel. The Catholic wedding was slated for ten o'clock. I was dressed in a black tuxedo, white shirt, black bow tie, and my black, shiny military shoes, the shoes we soldiers wear with our formal Class A and/or dress blue uniforms.

I picked up my parents at the hotel. My mom was wearing a nice, light-colored woman's suit appropriate for the occasion. My dad, who was still looking well at eighty-three, was wearing a nice blue suit. My parents hopped in my car, a silver Saturn sedan. Twenty minutes later, we reached the Church of the Risen Savior. I parked the car, and we all got out.

I started walking toward the church. After just a few steps, I felt a strange feeling under my feet.

What the heck? I'm walking, but my balance is off.

I kept walking, but my balance got progressively worse. My feet hit the asphalt unevenly, making me shift to the left and to the right. I looked down at my shoes, and I saw globs of black rubber. I looked behind me and saw a trail of black rubber steps leading to my car.

Oh no.

I immediately knew what happened. The black rubber soles of my military shoes were disintegrating with every step I took. Patches of black rubber lay on the asphalt, marking my previous steps.

My soles are disintegrating. But why?

Then it hit me.

I haven't worn my military dress shoes in years. The black rubber of my soles just got old and crumbled with my walking.

"Mom and Dad, I gotta go back to my apartment."

"Why?" asked my mother, all concerned. "The wedding is in forty-five minutes."

"My shoes are falling apart." I then pointed at the trail of evidence.

"Oh my," Mom said.

My dad started laughing.

"I have another pair of black shoes, but I have to go to my apartment."

"Why didn't you wear those black shoes instead of the ones you now have on?" my mom asked.

"Well, my military shoes are shinier and—"

"Just go and change your shoes," my mom told me. "And hurry. You don't want to be late for your wedding. I'll stay here because we have to do some decorations in the church."

Dad and I got into my car. As soon as I sat in the driver's seat, I noticed a glob of black rubber on the floor board next to the brake and accelerator pedals.

What a time to have my shoes disintegrate on me.

I started the car, pulled out of the church's parking lot, and raced to my apartment to change my shoes. My dad laughed and told jokes about my shoes during the entire trip.

*   *   *

I arrived at the church just in time for the wedding. It was hot, and I was sweating—the sweat probably caused more by my concern for being late than the hot weather. Dad took his seat next to my mom, and I went to the back of the church to meet the priest and my best man.

I had selected one of my law school buddies, a great and sharp guy named Brian, to be my best man. Brian and his lovely wife, Laura, have three kids. As a lawyer based in his native El Paso, Brian had passed both the Texas and New Mexico bar exams, the latter of which we had taken at the same time in Albuquerque.

"Glad to see you made it," the priest said, smiling, as I reached the back room of the church.

"Yes, Father." I proceeded to tell him about the shoe mishap.

He laughed. So did Brian. I then heard organ music.

"Okay, Paul. Are you ready for this?" asked the priest.

I responded confidently, "Yes, I am, Father."

The priest led the way, and Brian and I followed in tow. We were walking toward the base of the altar. To the right, on the church benches, I could see the small crowd of attendees/guests: my parents; my sister, Emily; her husband, John; John's parents; invitees from Prema's law firm; and instructors and associates from Latika's PhD/MBA program. Unfortunately, Latika's parents weren't able to get a tourist visa to attend our weddings.

With soft organ music playing, our trio of me, Brian, and the priest continued walking slowly. When we reached the base of the altar, the priest instructed Brian and me to turn and face the middle aisle.

The Church of the Risen Savior was one of those newer, modern Catholic churches with plenty of wide, empty spaces and high ceilings. Such a church reflected an architectural trend of the 1970s and 1980s, and it was in contrast to the two-story cathedrals built in the 1800s featuring old, wooden pews, narrow aisles, Roman-style columns, and thick, wooden podiums. That was what I was used to as a boy growing up in northern Maine. The church in our small town was built in the 1840s.

The organist changed melody, and with the new melody playing, I saw Latika, dressed in a beautiful white wedding dress with full veil, being escorted by Bill, Prema's husband. Prema and Bill filled in for Latika's parents. The center aisle was short but very wide. In a few moments, Latika and I were standing side by side. I shook hands with Bill, thanked him, and took my spot next to Latika. We were both facing the priest. The organ music stopped.

"We are gathered here today to celebrate the sacrament of marriage between Latika and Paul," the priest said in a loud voice. "Let us begin our celebration in the name of the Father and of the Son and of the Holy Spirit."

With those words, we all proceeded to do our signs of the cross, touching our foreheads, chests, left shoulders, and then right shoulders with our right hands.

The priest made more introductory remarks, and then we were instructed to sit down. Latika and I sat in two adjacent chairs to our left while Brian and Prema, the maid of honor, sat in the nearby church pew. It was time for the reading.

The topic of the reading from Scripture involved two decisions: what will the reading be and who will read it? Both of these decisions were no-brainers for me because I knew I wanted the reading where it is written, "Love is patient. Love is kind." I had told this to the priest some two weeks earlier.

"That's an excellent choice, Paul. It's a popular reading for weddings."

"Yes, Father. I'm not sure what part of the Bible it's from, but I remember the 'love is patient and love is kind' phrase. My sister, Emily, had read that passage at my first wedding."

"Indeed," said the priest, "it's from 1 Corinthians 13."

The second decision vis-à-vis the reading involved the reader. Who would do the reading? It was another no-brainer because I again selected Emily for this role.

Emily, dressed in a nice white and pink dress, walked up to the podium which was adjacent to the altar. The Bible, opened to the correct passage, was supported by the podium.

What follows is the reading Emily read, 1 Corinthians 13. There are different versions of this passage depending on whether one is using the Protestant or Catholic texts. For matters of research, I've selected the Protestant version, which closely parallels and is nearly verbatim to what Emily read at our wedding:

> *If I speak in the tongue of men and angels, but have not love, I am only a resounding gong or a clanging cymbal. If I have the gift of prophecy and can fathom all mysteries and all knowledge, and if I have a faith that can move mountains, but have not love, I am nothing. If I give all I possess to the poor, and surrender my body to the flame, but have not love, I again have nothing. Love is patient, love is kind. It does not envy, it does not boast, it is not proud. It is not rude, it is not self-seeking, it is not easily angered, it keeps no record of wrongs. Love does not delight in evil, but rejoices with the truth. It always protects, always trusts, always hopes, always perseveres. Love never fails. But where there are prophecies, they will cease; where there are tongues, they will be stilled; where there is knowledge, it will pass away. For we know in part and we prophecy in part, but when perfection comes, the imperfect disappears. When I was a child, I thought like a child, I reasoned like a child. When I became a man, I put childish ways behind me. Now we see but a poor reflection*

as in a mirror; then we shall see face to face. Now I know in part; then I shall know fully, even as I am fully known. And now these three remain: faith, hope and love. But the greatest of these is love.

After the reading, Emily stepped down from the podium. Then the priest walked down and stood next to myself and Latika. The priest spoke some ten minutes on the topic of the reading, love. He said how love is not always easy. For it to survive, there must be commitment and seriousness.

After his sermon, he asked Latika and I to stand. It was time for us to exchange our vows. I went first, repeating what the priest was saying.

"I, Paul, take you, Latika, to be my wife. I promise to be true to you in good times and in bad, in sickness and in health. I will honor you and love you all the days of my life."

"I, Latika, take you, Paul, to be my husband. I promise to be true to you in good times and in bad, in sickness and in health. I will honor you and love you all the days of my life."

Next, as is the tradition, came the exchange of rings, the symbol of our love and commitment to one another. Brian, standing to my immediate right, held the rings. I proceeded to place Latika's ring on her finger.

"Latika, take this ring as a sign of my love."

Latika then did the same. She placed my ring on my ring finger. "Paul, take this ring as a sign of my love."

The priest then instructed us to sign the marriage certificate that was placed on the altar. We did. Then we were instructed to sit in our chairs. Soft organ music started playing.

"For the Catholics in attendance, we will give Communion," announced the priest.

With that, a small line began to form in the short center aisle. I was the first to take Communion. Latika, a non-Catholic, stayed seated in her chair. I'm guessing roughly half of the guests were Catholics who took Communion.

The organ stopped playing.

The priest, now standing next to myself and Latika, said, "Please stand."

Everyone did. There was a pause.

Then the priest said, "Ladies and gentlemen, the ceremony is over. Please join me in welcoming Mr. and Mrs. Paul Bouchard. What God has joined, man cannot divide."

There was applause. Then the organ started playing again. I escorted my bride down the center aisle.

Following the Mass came photos, photos and more photos. Latika and I had hired a professional photographer, and he started directing traffic for the shots he was after.

"Okay, just the bride and groom at the altar."

"Now bride and groom with groom's family."

"Now the bride and groom with the bride's family."

"Okay, now just the groom and his best man."

"Let's follow that up with the bride and maid of honor."

And on it went like this for nearly an hour.

Our Catholic reception was at the Hyatt in downtown Albuquerque. We had a deejay who, per our instructions, played our favorite songs, mostly from the singer, Sade. The menu was Italian, alcoholic beverages were served,[16] and the conversations flowed. Then Brian, sharp as always, had some kind words as my best man.

More polite conversations and thank-yous ensued. Then it eventually came time for the slicing of the wedding cake. Latika and I had chosen a master baker, an elderly woman originally from England, to bake our special cake. The three-layer cake was full of chocolate and heavy on raspberries as well. It looked great, almost a work of art that was too nice to slice and eat. But, duties being duties, Latika and I sliced the top tier layer and ate the ceremonial pieces of cake. Shortly thereafter came the ceremonial first dance. Sade music played in the background.

What started around ten o'clock ended around six o'clock. The Catholic wedding and its reception was over. I drove my parents to their hotel, and then I went to my apartment. Latika stayed at Prema's house for there was lots of preparatory work needed for the following day's Hindu wedding.

Back at my apartment, I changed into my workout clothes and I went for a jog. I then showered and watched a ballgame on TV. I drank a beer while catching a few innings of the baseball game. Then I went to sleep. I slept well.

---

[16] Latika and her sisters, as good Hindus, didn't partake in alcohol.

CHAPTER SIX

The Hindu Wedding

At Open Seed University in Albuquerque at ten o'clock on August 21, 2004, we had our Hindu wedding. I was dressed in a maroon *kurta*, essentially a long tunic top for men. My *kurta* had a shine to it. My pants, cream-colored and loose-fitting, were made of cotton, and the beige shoes I had on my feet were thin and lightweight. As instructed, I wore no socks.

Open Seed University had an old warehouse, ill-kept feel to it. The building's outer walls were corrugated metal and beige in color. Patches of peeling paint were easily visible on many parts of these walls. Surrounding the building were gray, crushed rocks with weeds interspersed in the rocks. The only new-looking portion of the facility was its black asphalt driveway. It looked fresh and not dulled by sun or weathered with cracks.

The building's outer structure and grounds, however, didn't give the facility justice for inside, Open Seed University was clean, spacious, and nicely carpeted, giving it a modern classroom setting look. Latika and I had rented this facility, which offered classes devoted to Eastern spiritualism, languages, and philosophy, along with yoga and certain martial arts. Latika and I also paid a Hindu priest, a Cha Cha Gi, to officiate our wedding.

I had picked up my parents at their hotel, and then we drove across the Rio Grande River to the west side of Albuquerque. We reached Open Seed University in some twenty minutes.

Dressed in the traditional Hindu wedding attire, I exited my car, as did my parents. I started heading toward the building's main entrance. My parents were wearing similar, yet different, Western suits like they had worn the previous day for our Catholic wedding. My turban, the traditional male headgear, was, like my *kurta*, maroon in color. I was holding it in my right hand as I was walking.

56

As I approached the wide concrete walkway that led to the building's entrance, I noticed it was covered with bright flower petals—red, yellow, purple, and white in color. Written on the walkway were the words "Welcome." I figured the writing was made of chalk, but Latika later informed me the words "Welcome" were written using a white powder. The writings themselves were called *rangoli*.

My parents and I entered the building. Once inside, they proceeded to sit in the main room, the facility's largest room where the ceremony would take place, while I entered a small classroom off to the side. Earlier in the week, per instructions from Cha Cha Gi, I was instructed not to hang around the main lobby for fear of seeing my bride-to-be.

I sat quietly in the room and placed the turban on a nearby table. I was calm and relaxed. The ceremony would start in about forty-five minutes.

Some ten minutes passed. Then a short, middle-aged Indian man entered the small room I occupied. The man was thin, balding, and bespectacled. He was also dressed in white, loose clothing that resembled a *kurta*. He took a seat opposite of mine.

"Blessings to you, young man," he told me.

Like many Indians, his English was good, but spoken quite rapidly by Western standards.

"And to you, too," I responded.

"Thank you," he said. "It is my estimation that you are the one who is getting married. Is it so?"

"Yes, sir," I said. "I'm getting married today."

"This is most wonderful," he said in a serious manner. "I wish you good health and good blessings for this most important of events. It is truly a most auspicious day."

"Thank you," I said.

The Indian man shifted in his seat. "I am one of the instructors here at Open Seed University."

"I see. That's nice."

"Yes, thank you. It is my wish that the gods, the stars, and the universe are in balance for this auspicious day. This I tell you, good blessings to you once again."

"Thank you, sir. Thank you."

There was silence for just a few seconds.

"The problem in this great country, the United States, is the mind. The mind of the people is off. And the typical response to these mind problems is drugs. Drugs and pills and medicines."

I was listening with interest.

What the hell? There's still more than a half hour before the wedding kicks off.

"Yes, the American solution to everything is drugs and pills. One is depressed, give him drugs. One has learning disabilities, give him drugs. But my young man, I tell you this. The mind is not cured by drugs, for one must get to the source of the problem and simply not address the symptom."

"I see."

"The problem is one of the mind, one of attitude." The man's eyes got wider. "You see, one must understand that he is part of the universe and must thus become one with the universe. The answer is to accept life as it is and do the best one can with the help of universal energy."

"I see."

I think this guy is arguing the karma thing. Karma. Destiny.

"Drugs do not solve the issue, for one must be in balance with the universe."

"Okay."

There was silence. Then the man asked when I was born and Latika's date of birth.

I told him.

About ten seconds later, he said, "I am of the opinion that this marriage with your wife is meant to be."

"Thank you."

"What is the name of your bride?"

I told him.

"Ah, Sreenivasulu. That is Telegu. Your wife speaks Telegu. She is from the South. Around Madras, is it not so?"

*   *   *

I looked at my watch. There were five minutes before the wedding started. I stood up and placed the turban on my head. I could tell the main room was filling up because I was hearing the rumbling of people walking and conversing nearby.

Bill entered the room. "Paul, it is time."

I exited the small room and stood near the entrance of the main room. Recorded Hindustani music, with its fast-paced guitar and percussion sounds, played in the background. High-pitched female voices sang the lyrics.

Then, all of a sudden, I saw a man dressed in a white *kurta* blow into a large seashell, the sound produced being a loud horn sound. I walked forward and entered the main room which was essentially packed. All eyes were on me.

I took a few steps. Prema approached me and proceeded to make a *sindur*, a red dot made of reddish *sindur* powder, on my forehead. The man in the white *kurta* stood next to Prema, and he kept blowing into the seashell horn. Then Prema placed a beautiful garland of flowers around my neck, flowers that were white and maroon in color.[17]

I kept walking forward until I was instructed by a lady, the lady who had introduced myself and Latika to Cha Cha Gi, to simply stand at the base of what was a raised floor. I did as instructed and turned to face the crowd. The room, probably seating forty people, was full. I couldn't help but notice the interior light blue walls of this room being filled with paintings and posters of Ganesha, the half-man, half-elephant god of new beginnings, wisdom, and prosperity. I also noticed a trail of flower petals covering the carpeted main room.

The man in the white *kurta* kept blowing in the seashell horn. Then I noticed Latika entering the room. To her sides were two of her sisters. To her front was Prema, who proceeded to perform *arthi*, the removing of bad spirits by making the *bhindi*, the placing of the red dot on Indian females' foreheads.

After Prema placed the *bhindi* on Latika's forehead, Latika walked forward and eventually stood next to me. A garland, identical to mine, was around her neck.

My bride was dressed in a gorgeous gold and maroon sari. Every inch of her body, save her beautiful Halle Barry face, was covered with something. On her ears were huge gold earrings hanging down a few

---

[17] Latika specifically ordered all the flowers and garlands for our Hindu wedding from an Indian company based in Queens, New York. With seriousness and precision, the garlands and most of the flowers arrived the morning of our wedding. The garlands were made of roses and jasmine flowers.

inches. Her hands, dark brown in color, were covered with the traditional mehndi/henna. Her jet-black head of hair had a large jewelry ornament piece called a head tikka, which was gold in color. On both her wrists were gold bangles, so many in number that they almost reached her elbows.

The seashell horn stopped blowing, and then we were instructed to exchange our identical garlands three times. I placed my garland around Latika's neck, then she placed hers around my neck. The instructions came from the lady who had introduced us to Cha Cha Gi. She was wearing a beautiful, light pink sari.

After the exchange of garlands, the lady told us, "Walk up the three short steps of the raised floor, and take your places across from Cha Cha Gi and Cha Cha Gi's wife."

Latika and I did as instructed.

Suddenly, I heard Prema, who was standing behind me, say, "Paul, remove your shoes."

I then realized that Latika, all her sisters, the lady in the light pink sari, Cha Cha Gi, and his wife, were all barefoot. I removed my shoes and followed Latika up the short three steps. Across from us were Cha Cha Gi and his wife, and directly at our feet, spread out on the carpeted floor, were numerous silver trays and platters filled with colored powders, various-colored flower petals, white and yellow rice, incense, some dark brown coconuts, some water, a box of matches, a gold candleholder, and bright yellow bananas. With all that, however, the bright flower petals dominated most of the silver platters/trays.

Cha Cha Gi, a short, thin, bespectacled man in his early seventies, instructed Latika and I to sit down Indian-style in front of the silver trays and platters. He and his wife of similar age were directly across from us, and they were already sitting down Indian-style.

Cha Cha Gi instructed us to take the small tray of water and pour some water into our cupped hands. Latika and I did this. Then Cha Cha Gi grabbed a black microphone and proceeded to chant certain hymns. The hymns included several "om" and "uumn" sounds. Cha Cha Gi then drank some water from his cupped hands and told Latika and I to do the same. We did.

Cha Cha Gi carefully grabbed a bright yellow flower petal. He told us to do what he did, so Latika and I each grabbed a yellow flower petal from one of the trays before us. Cha Cha Gi then proceeded to touch his mouth and his right ear with the flower petal, and Latika and I, following suit, did the same.

Cha Cha Gi then grabbed the black microphone. "This is the invitation to all gods." His voice wasn't loud, but it was loud enough. He then broke out into certain hymns.

Latika told me that the hymns were in Sanskrit, an extremely old language. I didn't understand the hymns, but I noticed a lot of "hala" sounds and "uumn" sounds, too. Cha Cha Gi was reciting these with a certain rhythm, almost like a trance.

The lady in the light pink sari bent down and lit the incense that was situated in one of the silver platters. Immediately, smoke from the incense began to rise, and its pleasant smell spread quickly.

Cha Cha Gi then instructed us to take more flower petals from one of the platters and hold them in our right hands. "This is to worship all the planets."

Then he broke out into more hymns.

"Oohs" and "uumn" sounds ensued.

"Take more petals," he said.

We did.

"Now you both must place the petals in this platter." He pointed to the receiving platter. "You must now place flower petals into that platter nine times. Nine petals into the platter."

Latika and I did as instructed.

More hymns and chants from Cha Cha Gi ensued. I was focused, paying attention. I also began to feel pain in my right hip as it had been a long time since I had last sat Indian-style.

"Sa, Sa-lah, um-yah. We worship you," Cha Cha Gi said. "Be near to us."

There were more chants from Cha Cha Gi. The incense smell was getting stronger, too.

"We now offer water." Cha Cha Gi pointed for Latika and I to pour a bit of water into the platter containing our numerous flower petals.

We did this. Then Cha Cha Gi broke out into more hymns.

After some twenty seconds of hymns, Cha Cha Gi handed Me and Latika a cup of milk.

"Now take some of this, and place it in the platter with the flowers and the water."

We did as instructed.

There were more hymns from Cha Cha Gi and further instructions on the need to place more flower petals into the platter. Latika and I placed more flowers into the platter. Then Cha Cha Gi reached and grabbed a Tupperware container that I hadn't noticed. He handed us the container. It was filled with white squares.

Prema, sitting behind us, said, "Paul, the white squares are sweets."

Cha Cha Gi said, "Take one of the white squares in your right hand. Not your left hand, but your right hand."

Latika and I each took a white square. It reminded me of fudge.

"The sweets are for a prosperous, happy life," Cha Cha Gi told us. "Place your squares into the platter." He then started chanting in Sanskrit for a while. "Light the candle."

The gold candleholder and candle in it were next to Latika. The lady in the light pink sari proceeded to light the candle.

"Both of you pick up the candleholder," Cha Cha Gi said after the candle was lit, "and make small circles with it."

I wasn't sure what he meant, but Latika luckily had the lead. She started making small circular rotations with the candleholder. I just held on to the candleholder and allowed her to do the rotations.

"We will now offer milk to the gods," Cha Cha Gi said. He instructed us to place the candleholder and its candle next to a platter. Then he told us to reach out with cupped hands. He proceeded to pour milk into our cupped hands.

"Drink the milk in your hands," he said.

We did. Then Cha Cha Gi poured water into our cupped hands.

"The water is to wash your hands." He started chanting. The chanting lasted about ten seconds or so. "Now place your hands on the candleholder again, for we must get the energy from the gods."

We did as instructed.

"We will now perform the *khanyandan*," the lady in the light pink sari said loudly. "This is when the daughter is given to the groom."

Prema and Bill, filling in for Latika's parents, stood up from their chairs. They were holding a silver platter filled with bright flower petals.

"With your right hands, not your left, hold the bride's right hand," Cha Cha Gi told Prema and Bill.

They did as instructed. Cha Cha Gi then told me to also hold Latika's right hand, and I did.

"I am giving my daughter," he told Prema and Bill, "my well-educated, my well-loved daughter to you." As he said "you," he looked at me. I nodded in approval.

Cha Cha Gi then started chanting. At one point, he told Prema to repeat after him.

"Om."

"Om."

"Da ta to Om."

"Da ta to Om."

"Do la a shum."

"Do la a shum."

And on it went like this with Prema not missing a beat.

Cha Cha Gi then looked at me. "Say what I say."

Oh no. Hey, I'm not as good as Prema.

"Om."

I said something that sounded like "Om."

"Swuchap."

I said something that sounded like what I just heard.

Just think phonics. Think phonics.

"Sto-rie."

I did my best impression of "sto-rie."

"Shan-ti."

I gave my best recital of "Shan-ti."

"What I just told you means I accept your offer," Cha Cha Gi told me. "I accept your offer of our daughter."

I nodded in approval. There was silence. Then the lady in the light pink sari started applauding. Everyone in the room followed suit. Next, I noticed Bharathi, one of Latika's sisters, take a platter that was next to myself and Latika. The platter contained a coconut and a string, more like a thread. Bharathi started passing around that platter to the crowd of attendees.

"The platter is being passed around to get the blessing of the people," said Cha Cha Gi as the platter was making its rounds.

Suddenly, I heard the horn sound again. Sure enough, the man who had previously blown into the seashell horn was once again doing that task.

I was still sitting Indian-style, and my right hip was killing me.

This ceremony, this wedding, is easily twice or three times longer than yesterday's wedding. This is cool, all new to me, but my hip is killing me.

The seashell horn stopped playing, and then the lady in the light pink sari lit a small fire next to myself and Latika. A small iron bowl was filled with thin, wooden pieces. That's what the lady lit—the wooden pieces. Cha Cha Gi started chanting again.

Surprisingly, in a short period of time, maybe thirty seconds or so, I noticed the small fire beginning to be not so small at all. Somehow, its flames grew in size, and I could feel the fire's heat. Latika and I, still sitting Indian-style, backed up some two feet.

The lady in the light pink sari handed me a silver platter. Inside the platter was a small container filled with a dark brown powder. I was instructed to place some of this brown powder into the fire. I did so, and the addition produced a crackling sound and a few sparks.

"Now it is time for the seven vows," the lady said. "Stand up."

"We will have to walk around the fire seven times, Paul," Latika whispered to me as she stood next to me.

"Good," I whisperedd to her. "My right hip is killing me from all the Indian-style sitting, but standing up feels better. I think walking will help."

The lady in the light pink sari then reached for the back side of my *kurta*. This particular portion of the *kurta* is called the *duppatta*. The lady proceeded to tie the *duppatta* to Latika's sari. Once that was done, Bharathi, who stood between myself and Latika, placed a coconut where the tie knot was.

"Paul, you will now lead," the lady said. "Start walking around the fire, and your bride will follow. Don't worry. The coconut between you two will not fall off."

I followed orders and started walking around the small but growing fire with Latika in tow. Sure enough, the coconut in between held steady.

"The first encirclement is for prosperity," the lady said for all in the audience to hear.

Cha Cha Gi started chanting. I kept walking slowly, my eyes fixated on the fire so I wouldn't accidentally fall into it. I forget what the other encirclements stood for vows-wise, but I had the lead for the first three encirclements.

Then the lady said, "Now Latika will lead."

Latika walked in front of me and took the lead. She did lead for the last four encirclements.

"Now the brother must give away his sister," the lady said.

Latika started leading for the last encirclement. Given that Latika's only brother wasn't able to attend our wedding, Prema's and Bill's son, Vijay, filled that role. Cha Cha Gi gave him some rice, and he was instructed to throw the rice at Latika as she walked around the fire.

"The giving of rice symbolizes that he has given away his sister," Cha Cha Gi said as Vijay threw some rice at his aunt.

"And now you must walk around the fire another seven times," Cha Cha Gi told Latika and I just as we were finishing our seventh encirclement.

What? Another seven times? When in Rome, do as the Romans. Plus walking feels better than sitting Indian-style.

Latika and I walked around the fire another seven times, with Latika in lead. The purpose of these last seven encirclements was never explained to us, but, this time, the lady instructed us to throw rice into the fire. We did as instructed.

"Please, now sit," Cha Cha Gi said as we finished the last encirclement.

The coconut in between myself and Latika was removed. We sat down again, Indian-style. The pain in my right hip resumed, but it wasn't as bad as before, given the therapeutic affect of the walking.

"Please, take some of this red powder," Cha Cha Gi told me, handing me a platter that held the powder. "And make a red line in the center of your bride's hairline and forehead." I reached for some powder and started placing it on Latika's center hairline, but Prema, sensing I was probably too cautious and slow, helped me with this task, which took maybe fifteen seconds.

"Now take the *thali*, Paul, and tie it around your bride's neck," Cha Cha Gi told me.

The *thali* was the thread that was in the platter along with the coconut. It was handed to me, and I proceeded to tie it loosely around Latika's neck with relative ease and quickness.

Next, Cha Cha Gi said, "Now, Paul, place these on your bride's toes." He handed me two small gold rings.

I knelt down. With some difficulty, I placed the rings on two of Latika's toes. When I was pushing the last ring up on one of Latika's toes, I heard the lady in the light pink sari tell the audience, "You may throw flower petals on the couple." Some of our guests did just that.

"And now we will do the *ashirwad*," the lady said seconds after I had placed the rings on Latika's toes.

I later found out *ashirwad* means the "blessing of the elders."

Cha Cha Gi instructed Prema and Bill to step forward. Then he told me and Latika to bow down at their feet.

"Now you two," Cha Cha Gi said, referring to Prema and Bill, "you bend down and touch the backs of the newlyweds." Bill and Prema did as told. They bent down and touched our backs as we were bowing down in front of them.

"And now the parents of the groom," Cha Cha Gi announced.

My mother walked forward.

Where's Dad?

My eighty-three-year-old father was nowhere in the audience.

"Your dad left this room, Paul," my mother said as she walked up in front of me. "He couldn't take all the smoke in this room. You know he has asthma."

So that explained it. Dad couldn't take all the smoke. No worries though as my mom did this blessing all by herself. She stood in front of me and Latika. We bowed down, and she touched our backs.

After my mother walked off, the lady in the light pink sari said loudly, "I now present you Mr. and Mrs. Paul Bouchard." The audience applauded.

*   *   *

Latika and I had a short reception at Open Seed University following our wedding there. The menu was Indian, the music was Hindustani, and there was no alcohol.

Looking back, I'd say the Hindu wedding was at least three times longer than our Catholic one. I had never attended a Hindu wedding before. The attire, music, chants, throwing of rice, flower petals, milk, water, walking around a fire seven times with a coconut in between you and your bride, bowing down at your parents, and making of a red line on your wife's hairline and forehead—all of this was new to me, so of course I found it very ritualistic.

Then again, as I reflect on the two ceremonies, I asked myself a key question—What was the Catholic ceremony for Latika? Latika had never attended a Catholic wedding. The white gown, flowers, sign of the cross, commands of sitting, kneeling, or standing, reading from the Bible, signing of the marriage certificate, soft organ music, and giving of Communion—all of those things were new to Latika just as *kurtas*, *thalis*, and *ashirwad* were new to me. We had planned to have a Catholic wedding and a Hindu wedding, and that's what took place. And I'm glad we did because we had two nice ceremonies.

CHAPTER SEVEN

Final Thoughts

Latika and I have been married for five years as of this writing, and I can honestly say it has been a good five years. Sure, we've had our down moments. "Love is patient. Love is kind. It keeps no record of wrongs." But mostly it has been ups. This East-meets-West union is working, and I'm glad for it.

Undoubtedly, I've noticed some Westernizing of Latika since our courtship and eventual marriage. She now speaks English a tad slower, and she continually incorporates American slang into her vocabulary, like saying high five and cool. What follows are three important events that have happened to my wife since we met:

- Latika has learned to drive a car, and she has obtained her driver's license.
- Latika became an American citizen in 2008. She tells me that, next to our marriage, her obtaining American citizenship was one of the happiest days in her life. She is very proud to be an American.
- Latika has obtained an American government job at the military base where I'm stationed. Not only is she proud to be a citizen, she's equally proud to work for the government of her new citizenship.

Importantly, however, I am of the opinion that, though she is Westernizing and Americanizing, my wife will always retain and exhibit some aspects of the Indian culture she grew up with. These include:

- Cuisine
- My wife likes many cuisines, but Indian, especially South Indian, will always be her favorite. Also, like many Indians, Latika doesn't like to have ice in her water.

- ◆ Music
- ◆ Latika loves Western music. George Michael, Abba, Michael Jackson, and Sade are some of her favorites, but she'll always prefer Indian music. She likes some Japanese musicians as well.
- ◆ The Seriousness, Ambition, and Money-oriented Aspect of Indians
- ◆ I discussed these topics in some detail in this book, and Latika certainly has these traits. She has two graduate degrees, and she's very focused on moving up the government job ladder. She's focusing on promotions: how much they pay and what she needs to do to obtain them. She's also a bad tipper and a tough-as-nails negotiator. Latika constantly asks for monetary discounts, and she dutifully and meticulously reviews each and every receipt to ensure we haven't been overcharged.
- ◆ The Reservations of the Indian People
- ◆ Latika's friendly, but not overly so. She's hesitant to invite anyone in our home who she doesn't know well. And unlike me, where I'm always talking to taxi drivers when in a taxi, Latika never talks to taxi drivers. I find that Indians, in general, are suspicious of others, and they generally have a distrustful nature.

As for India, all I know about it is what I read about it and what Latika tells me when we discuss the subject. I know it's:

- ◆ Heavily populated
- ◆ Has some fifteen hundred languages
- ◆ Is the second-largest Muslim country in the world
- ◆ Is the largest democracy in the world
- ◆ Is growing rapidly in an economic sense
- ◆ Has a lot of poverty

Here's a description of India as written in the May 23-29, 2009, issue of *The Economist*. The article is entitled "Good News: Don't Waste It."

India is a land of bright promise. It is also extremely poor. About 2.7 million Indians will be born this year. Unless things improve, almost two million of them will die before the next general election. Of the children who survive, more than 40 percent will be physically stunted by malnutrition.

> *Most will enroll in a school, but they cannot count on their
> teachers showing up. After five years of classes, less than 60
> percent will be able to read a short story, and more than 60
> percent will still be stumped by simple arithmetic.*

The article goes on to say that, because many Indians are illiterate, political parties must use a symbol, such as a flower, bow and arrow, ceiling fan, or cricket player, to symbolize their political party so the voters will know which symbol to select when they are voting. I've heard similar tales of this illiteracy factor for other countries such as Pakistan and Bangladesh.

The Economist article, in my opinion, stands in stark contrast to the Indian experience here in America. Consider the Indians who come to America and become successful in the hotel business or convenience store business, or the educated Indians who do very well here as professors, scientists, software engineers, and medical doctors. Not too long ago, a friend of mine informed me that, if you break down Americans into ethnic groups, the second-highest income earners in America, second only to Jews, are Indians. If that's not proof of the seriousness, ambition, and money-oriented nature of Indians, I don't know what is.

I've never been to India, though I've written about it in this book. Such a fact reminds me of what my favorite writer, Michael Crichton, once wrote in his excellent book, *Travels*. "The only true experience is direct experience."

Crichton was right, which is why I hope to visit India some day, to get that direct experience of seeing the sights, smelling the smells, and experiencing it all. I'm looking forward to such a trip, and I plan on taking plenty of photographs. I even plan on speaking Indian English.

"Pass the film roll, please."

ABOUT THE AUTHOR

Paul Bouchard is an Army JAG lawyer who began his military career as an Army reporter. His books include *Enlistment* and two novellas, *The Boy Who Wanted to Be a Man* and *A Package at Gitmo*. For more on Paul Bouchard visit www.authorpaulbouchard.com.

www.ingramcontent.com/pod-product-compliance
Lightning Source LLC
Chambersburg PA
CBHW020339290526
45785CB00005B/2086